T0195007

AN EDUCATOR'S GUIDE TO PERSONAL PRIDE

How To Survive Discrimination and
Find Success in Your Career

LARRY PLUMMER

Author of
"The Force Behind the Dream"

AN EDUCATOR'S GUIDE TO PERSONAL PRIDE
HOW TO SURVIVE DISCRIMINATION AND
FIND SUCCESS IN YOUR CAREER

iUniverse books may be ordered through booksellers or by contacting:

iUniverse
1663 Liberty Drive
Bloomington, IN 47403
www.iuniverse.com
844-349-9409

Because of the dynamic nature of the Internet, any web addresses or links contained in this book may have changed since publication and may no longer be valid. The views expressed in this work are solely those of the author and do not necessarily reflect the views of the publisher, and the publisher hereby disclaims any responsibility for them.

Any people depicted in stock imagery provided by Getty Images are models, and such images are being used for illustrative purposes only. Certain stock imagery © Getty Images.

ISBN: 978-1-6632-3712-5 (sc)
ISBN: 978-1-6632-3721-7 (hc)
ISBN: 978-1-6632-3713-2 (e)

Library of Congress Control Number: 2022904893

Print information available on the last page.

iUniverse rev. date: 05/17/2022

CONTENTS

PART 2

PREFACE

The fact of unfair dealings in the workplace should come as no surprise to any American. In fact, the history of labor and employment in our country is rife with stories of unfair treatment, favoritism, and/ or nepotism. Even though these occurrences are bad and pervasive enough in any workplace, they are especially egregious in public schools. This book's emphasis on unfair dealings as related to educational professionals is in no way an attempt to minimize or degrade the honest and productive work any person undertakes in any employment situation. It cannot be disputed, however, that there is a difference between a job and a career. A person seeking employment will want easy access to a job for decent wages. A person seeking a career will undertake a painstaking quest after years of training, including perhaps an internship and continuous study. This pursuit is usually engaged in by way of a profession. The pursuit and maintenance of a profession despite the barrage of potential obstructions that this book will reveal and discuss is this book's sole purpose.

When an individual undertakes to enter the profession of pedagogy, there are some realities. Even before being considered for a position as a professional in public schools, the potential candidate must undertake years of post-high school education and training. Often, the potential educator is obligated to sacrifice finances, time, and effort to obtain a bachelor's degree, which is the fundamental requirement for entry into the field of pedagogy. After having obtained the bachelor's degree in education, the potential teacher must then undertake training to obtain a certificate to engage in teaching. The education and training could result in a certificate in special education, education of the handicapped, kindergarten through eighth grade, kindergarten through twelfth grade, and several other different variations of certifications and endorsements.

Even after the potential educator obtains the bachelor's degree and then the certificate, the daunting task of obtaining a job is at the forefront of the next part of his or her ambition. The potential educator engages in several hours of examination, research, visits, networking, and other activities undertaken to find that first job. The ambitious educator writes résumés and curricula vitae; he or she sends them to several potential employers, thereby expending several hundreds of dollars in printing and copying fees and postage. The advent of online submission and filing ameliorates some of the costs. The savings are usually offset by the time expended and the equipment accessed to use this application device. Most often these efforts are met with no response at all. Many times, the response is a letter indicating that the potential employer isn't interested in the résumés submitted, but "thank you very much anyway."

The time may come when the letter in the mailbox from a potential employer indicates that the employer has expressed some interest in the candidacy of the person to whom the letter was sent. The employer asks the letter's recipient to call the school district to set up an appointment. This is wonderful news, and the potential teacher is overwhelmed with enthusiasm, runs to the telephone, and calls the district to set up an appointment. The candidate goes through his or her wardrobe, determines which outfit would be best for the interview, practices his or her best interview style, and does everything necessary to prepare for this hopefully life-changing event.

The big day arrives. The candidate goes into the office of the interviewer. In his or her mind, he or she runs through the appropriate way to sit, look, stand, and greet the interviewer—along with every other thing he or she believes he or she should know in order to be a successful candidate. The candidate cannot help but envision thoughts of success in this interview. He or she has daydreamed about being a teacher, going into the classroom, greeting his or her students, and being a benchmark for the profession. The school principal emerges from his or her office, walks up to the candidate, extends his or her hand, and ushers the candidate into his or her office.

If the candidate is successful, he or she will embark on and be introduced to a very noble profession. If the candidate acquits himself or herself in a professional, straightforward manner and does everything required of him or her in the profession, the candidate has a right to advance and excel in this noble endeavor. He or she has a right to have his or her efforts recognized and rewarded with greater responsibility and more leadership possibilities. Of course, this is dependent on the candidate's desire.

This book is dedicated to all those ambitious and motivated people who envision an entry into a thousand-year profession, whom some of the finest people in history have undertaken, shaped, molded and attempted to improve. It is also dedicated to the educators who have worked in the profession all their lives and have dedicated themselves to it. Finally, it is dedicated to an exposure of the practices of some highly placed professionals who openly or surreptitiously ignore and/ or thwart the efforts of potential educators to enter the field or to advance in it.

The book also provides a warning and an exposition of the unfortunate practices in which many school districts have engaged. These practices include advancing to greater leadership and more responsible positions only those individuals who have friends, relatives, or other connections in the district. These are persons known by the district and are popular in it, persons who are related to members of the community and are potentially possessed of significant local power from those who know how to play the game.

We should realize that public education had its origins in local communities and was created as a local phenomenon. The history of the profession indicates that teachers usually come from the communities in which they live. Teachers have usually attended school in the community in which they will later teach. The historical fact is that persons hired for positions in the municipality tend to be from the municipality. The Department of Public Works, the mayor's office, the tax assessor's office, the municipal court, the fire department, the police department, and local schools have historically hired locally. This is one of the bedrock reasons many were consistently shut out of positions in education. Many of these communities hired only those connected with or related to someone of prominence in the community or those of a certain race, religion, color, or other superficial identity.

A dedicated professional shouldn't be prevented from pursuing and advancing in his or her chosen profession because of subjective, biased, or racist reasons if he or she is qualified to enter the profession, advance in it, or both. The cost in finances, time, effort, and energy to enter and advance in the profession only makes fair and appropriate the recognition of those dedicated enough to extend themselves and make their service exemplary for the sake of the profession, the students or whomever they serve. A professional who constantly finds himself or herself shut out and ignored when opportunities for entry and/ or advancement arise for which he or she might be eminently qualified, must have recourse and be able to confront these issues. They must also be prepared to confront those dedicated to favoring others because of familial issues, race, nepotism, or other subjective reasons.

The purpose of this book is to expose the unfortunate proclivity of the power base of certain school districts to maintain in themselves a singular program of self-sustainment. This program exists at the expense of honorable and dedicated professionals who do not happen to "belong". While reading this book, keep in mind that it is all for our students and that the taking on, the retention and promotion of exemplary educational professionals ultimately benefits the children in our public schools.

INTRODUCTION

The genesis of discrimination, favoritism, and bias in hiring and promotion has its origin in the culture of early communities where the culture came to be accepted and developed and later, evolved into law. This is how segregated communities especially those in the north, came into existence. These segregated communities spawned generations of people who were born, were educated in, lived in, and spent their entire lives there. If the proposition is true that these communities hired local people for their local needs and the community itself worked to keep the community restricted, it's easy to see how those of another race, color, religion, ethnicity, or national origin had very little ability to break into any local organizations for employment including the local school district. It's easy to see that those who weren't favored in the community had a difficult, if not impossible time breaking into established institutions such as the public schools.

Given this backdrop and recognition of the fact that these communities were segregated (not only by race but by "pedigree" and connections) for decades, sometimes even centuries, it isn't difficult to understand that favoritism, nepotism, and the overall overt exclusion of outsiders in the hiring and promotion practices were allowed to exist and prevail in these communities. If the mayor of the town, whose daughter had just graduated from college, wanted his daughter to be a teacher, and the superintendent of schools had a wife who needed a secretarial position, and the mayor and the superintendent saw each other in church every Sunday and played golf every Wednesday, it isn't difficult to determine that conversations were held, and agreements were made. Given that scenario, outsiders had no place in this conversation and no ability to be treated fairly when seeking any of these positions.

The conversations, the gentlemen's agreements, and the understandings between prominent members of the community and other such nebulous interactions weren't the only or most effective way to keep assignments and positions open and available only to certain people. The written, codified, and statutory law played a significant part in assuring homogeneity in the hiring and promotion practices of communities. For several decades, the law allowed an assurance of exclusivity in the community, and community members rarely hesitated to enforce their discriminatory xenophobia. They often used the courts to keep their communities "pure." The primary, most powerful, and most effective legal device to assure quasi consanguinity and restriction in the community was an exclusion called the "restrictive covenant."

The legal document that is evidence of property transfer and ownership is called a "deed." Before 1948, a common clause in many deeds that assured a seller's (and a community's) guarantee that a community would remain the way the community members wanted it to be was a restrictive covenant. It is merely a promise that the purchaser of real property will engage in or refrain from engaging in certain acts on, with, or having to do with the property. Although a restrictive covenant can really restrict any action having to do with the land being purchased, for our purposes the restrictive covenant referred to here is the one that restricts the property seller from selling the property to members of certain races, religions, colors, national origins, and so forth.

Although the United States Supreme Court rendered it unconstitutional in the case of *Shelley v. Kramer*,[1] the restrictive covenant was widely used to establish and maintain the segregation of whole communities. Segregation, primarily in the South, was a de jure issue, meaning it was the law. In the north, however, segregation was de facto, meaning that although it wasn't the law of the municipality or the state, certain facts existed that made segregation a reality. One of these factors was the restrictive covenant.

So how did this restrictive covenant work? Let's say I want to buy a house. I go to the homeowner and say, "I want to buy your house." He says, "Fine." We engage in the usual prerequisites. I obtain a deed. The deed has a restrictive covenant in it. The restrictive covenant says I cannot sell my house or land to anyone who is six feet tall. Let's say I ignore the restrictive covenant and sell my house to someone who is six feet tall. If my neighbors or any member of the community finds out I have sold my property to someone who is six feet tall, that person can sue to have the transfer negated and require the seller to take back the property and me to take back the purchase price. This is what happened in the landmark Supreme Court case of *Shelley v. Kramer*.

In 1945, an African American family by the name of Shelley purchased a house in St. Louis, Missouri. There was a restrictive covenant attached to the deed that ran with the land. The Shelley's were unaware of this restrictive covenant; the covenant had been on the property since 1911. The restrictive covenant prevented "people of the Negro or Mongolian race from occupying the property." Louis Kramer, who lived ten blocks away from the subject property, sued to

---

[1] 334 U.S. 1 (1948).

prevent the Shelleys from gaining possession of the property. The case went all the way to the Missouri Supreme Court. That court ruled that the restrictive covenant was enforceable because it was purely a private agreement between its original parties, and as such it ran with the land.

The Shelley's petitioned the US Supreme Court for relief on the grounds of the Fourteenth Amendment guarantee of the equal protection of the laws. That provision, simply stated, guarantees that "all people similarly situated must be treated similarly."[2] The Shelleys' simple proposition was that if they had been white, all other things being equal, they would have been able to purchase the house. The US Supreme Court held that restrictive covenants standing alone cannot be regarded as a violation of any rights guaranteed to the petitioners (the Shelleys) by the Fourteenth Amendment. However, the court indicated that enforcement of such agreements couldn't be sought or obtained through state courts because such would be state action, and that would be violative of the Fourteenth Amendment. Consequently, restrictive covenants based on any of the protected categories, including race, color, or national origin, aren't enforceable in the courts of the United States, but they are perfectly legal if they remain private affairs.

The favoritism, racism, and nepotism I was the victim of in my more than twenty-five-year career in education was largely the result of the closed and exclusive proclivity of the community where I practiced my profession. I am not the only one who has been a victim; many educational professionals I have met during my tenure as an educator in my school district have regaled me with stories that indicated their victimization. When I first applied for a principalship, I had already served for four years as a vice principal. Although I was regularly and routinely the most qualified person applying, I had to apply fifteen

---

[2] **U.S. Const. amend. XIV, § 1**

times over fourteen years before I was successful in obtaining a principal position. This was in spite of the fact that, in a majority of the situations, I was the best and most highly qualified for the position.

I was the victim not only of race, age, and gender discrimination but also of favoritism, bias, and unfairness in the application process. I used every means at my disposal to realize my goals and actuate my dreams. No amount of entrenched unfairness was going to deter me from what I had trained and set my mind for. This book is a reflection of my experiences and is a clarion call to you for your success.

I have been told of qualified, long-term educational professionals who weren't endowed with connections or were the wrong color or ethnicity that had applied for administrative, and/ or supervisory positions and directorships. Not only were they not considered for these positions, but the school board engaged in a myriad of unethical and outrageous actions to thwart their candidacy, including, but not limited to withdrawing the position and reposted it in another name or designation. This step was taken just to keep that person from applying for it.

This is to introduce Andrew James Applicant, a dark-skinned, African American, born in Haiti and raised in Florida who possesses a slight accent. He graduated 1st in his class from Columbia University and is a member of Phi Beta Kappa. Andy Applicant was trying to break into the profession of pedagogy. He was applying for an initial position. It cannot be disputed that entry into a time-honored and noble profession such as education isn't easy. This is appropriate because only the brightest, best, and most motivated should be allowed to take their place in the classroom and mentor the most valuable entity our society possesses: its children. This doesn't mean, however, that ancillary, irrelevant, and inequitable forces can be brought to bear to stifle and/ or deny an otherwise-qualified candidate.

This book will also provide guidance for any educator who seeks higher and more responsible positions but because of some of the issues hereinbefore delineated was disallowed and nonselected for the positions notwithstanding his or her qualifications. To expound on the issue of an already-employed educator who seeks higher and more responsible positions and opportunities, you will meet Amy Maria Ambitious, a proud Latina who wants to improve her school district and students by moving into greater positions of authority.

The following pages will reveal Andy's and Amy's ordeals and how they dealt with them. It will be a primer showing how you might deal with blatant unfairness in the face of your attempt to secure a teaching job or to move to higher and more responsible positions in your school district. Andy and Amy discuss the items they drafted and used to obtain fairness, including filings, grievances, letters, complaints, briefs, memoranda of law, filings with the Equal Employment Opportunity Commission (EEOC), and many other items. They discuss these items related to their actions and will discuss courses of action you might pursue in the attempt to realize fairness, equity, and propriety when seeking recognition of your background, experience, credentials, and plain hard work.

Here is one final word in this introduction. You must not think it is vanity or self-centeredness if you speak up and demand fairness when dealing with your profession. Some might misunderstand these words to indicate a sense of entitlement. The purveyors of this point of view are generally those who have the positions you seek. These people are usually on the glide path of a position of authority and/or esteem because of their family, position, race, or something else that gets them a prime seat at the table.

Although this work describes the undertakings of fictional characters, they are all based on factual accounts of real people and actions they undertook to address them. There is nothing wrong with expounding your qualities and qualifications. There is nothing inappropriate with making yourself the very best you can be. When you seek greater experience, more formidable credentials, and more significant responsibility, you enhance not only yourself but also your profession; and the beneficiary of this attitude are those we seek to aid: our students.

Remember, silence is worse than acquiescence; it is an endorsement.

PART 1

1

PREPARATION, APPLICATION, AND REVIEW

The eager would-be educator must traverse several hurdles before walking into that first classroom as a teacher. He or she must first apply for the position. This is what Andrew James Applicant did. The eager educator will review several newspaper classified ads, go online, and cull the many positions offered. He or she will painstakingly consider all the requirements and job descriptions. A decision will be made as to which position should be applied for.

The application process for an educator is unlike most others. The application these days is primarily online and doesn't merely ask for name, address, telephone number, and educational qualifications and certifications. It asks questions about the applicant and his or her idea of education. The next few pages are dedicated to identifying some of the issues an applicant will be asked to address and suggestions regarding responses to them.

One favorite question contained in applications of school districts engaged in the hiring of teachers is "What is your teaching philosophy?"

This is a question you should give serious consideration to. You should always research the district you are applying to. This is especially true for a thorough and complete response to this question. This is because the district might have embarked on a program you would do well to mention or cite as part of your teaching philosophy. In any event, certain points should be included in all questions of this type. A recommended response to this type of question is located in Appendix A.

The items provided are merely suggestions. A candidate should never use someone else's work verbatim. A better practice is to take suggestions and mold them into his or her own work.

Another question that might be asked in an application, be the question verbal or written, is "How will you engage parents and the community in your teaching practice?" You would really impress the decision-makers if you not only specifically and succinctly expressed your intentions in this regard but also provided a month-by-month delineation of your proposed plan. That would be an eye-opener. A suggestion as to how to respond can be found in Appendix B.

Another common question in the application process is how you would deal with English language learners, gifted and talented students, and disabled students in your class. This area is very important given the ever-present and growing educational philosophy of inclusion of all students and having all students learn in the least restrictive environment. A suggestion for addressing this question can be found in Appendix C.

You will undoubtedly be asked what the characteristics of an excellent teacher are. More and more, teaching candidates are being confronted regarding what they believe the very definition of teaching is. They are being asked what things are necessary to create the consummate educator. The response to these queries must be expansive and not isolated. Present-day school and district administrators are looking for teachers who are conversant with the entire scope of education; that which extends outside the classroom. They want motivated professionals, those who are proactive, willing to go above and beyond, and dedicated to professional development for the sake of student achievement. A suggestion and possible response can be found in Appendix D.

You must provide more than just an answer to these or any other questions posed in the application process and/ or during the interview: you must exude confidence and definitiveness in your response. You must be enthusiastic about education, and this attitude must come through in your responses. The interviewer is looking for a teacher/ leader, someone who will enhance the quality of his or her building or school district. This desire emanates from the fact that the education of young people is becoming more an activity that exists and thrives outside the classroom. Administrators want someone who enters the building every day early and leaves late.

Interviewers are more than administrators; they are watchers. They watch teachers during the day. As a principal myself, I can attest to the fact that my evaluation of my teachers is more than just a product of their classroom performance, although that is still very important. I have always valued the volunteer for school dances, the faculty adviser for fundraising, the volunteer for special projects introduced at faculty meetings, and the questioner of materials and procedures. But along with them are those who don't just question and/or complain but arrive with solutions to issues. These issues, when addressed, take the candidate above and beyond all others.

It is almost certain that you will be asked to provide your opinion of technology in education. The genie of technology is out of the bottle, and it isn't going back in. Not only do we use technology in our instructional model, but school districts are rapidly providing personal computers, iPads, cell phones, and smart boards to teachers. Districts now provide personal computers to students in all grades from pre-kindergarten to twelfth grade.

Additionally, almost every student possesses his or her own cell phone, sometimes his or her own PCs, and many other devices. The explosion of social media is also an issue to be dealt with. The administrator will want to know not only how you intend to use technology in your classroom, if at all, but also how you will deal with students' personal devices that make appearances in the classroom. This is an issue you must give considerable thought to.

Finally, as related to the issue of technology, the administrator will want to know your proficiency in technology. He or she will be forward looking and expansive as it relates to this issue. He or she is going to want to know not only your proficiency but also your willingness to incorporate the use of technology in your instructional model. He or she will also be looking to see whether you can be a resource for technological support in the building. The administrator you apply to or face in the interview has a school with teachers who have been around for twenty years, thirty years, or more. The administrator will want someone able to work with these teachers and others.

The old-timers might resist technology, but the district cannot and will not. Those teachers who are there will need to acclimate themselves. The interviewer will look at you to provide some of these skills. Please review Appendix E.

A curveball question, one I have used in interviews and on applications I have conducted and sent to teaching candidates during my several years as a principal and vice principal, is "What is your idea of an excellent school principal and/or building administrator?" This is a modification of the interview-the-interviewer strategy, whereby the interviewer gleans information and an idea of the alternate philosophy of the candidate's pedagogical point of view. This is an easier question to answer on an application because one might think about it, then respond in writing.

This is a curveball question, because very few candidates for teaching positions believe they will be asked this during an interview; consequently, they are blindsided by it. Upon hearing the question, many candidates I interviewed gave me the deer-in-the-headlights stare, didn't respond at all, or did anything except answer the question. These responses are not only inappropriate because every teacher should have an idea of what he or she expects from the principal of the school where he or she will be employed, but also because a teacher should never be at a loss to answer any question. Suppose a student asked a question the teacher wasn't prepared to answer. Enough said.

In any event, the least the candidate might say if nothing comes to mind would be "This is a very interesting question, which I never thought of. I would like the opportunity to consider it and provide you with a written, follow-up response to this question. I will send it to you by email before the day is out." With this response, the interviewer won't get a direct response to the question but will know the candidate can think on his or her feet and is dexterous when confronted in an awkward situation.

I have provided a possible response to this question in Appendix F. These are some areas an administrator might consider important.

2

INTERVIEW, FOLLOW-UP, EMPLOYMENT, RETENTION AND PROMOTION

A ndy went on several interviews. The interviews resulting from the applications he had submitted had come to an end. Andy was feeling very good. He had answered the questions with directness and sincerity and in a style that bespoke his knowledge of the subject. The interviewers seemed to be receptive and pleased with Andy's responses.

Andy left the interviews with a spring in his step and hope in his heart. He had done everything correctly, including sending an email to the interviewers and thanking them for consideration. Andy had even been thoughtful enough to send a letter by regular mail, saying the same thing. Andy believed he had nailed it and anticipated that any day, even any moment, an employer would contact him and offer a position.

Then the stark reality came to light. One of two scenarios played out after the interviews. Either he wasn't contacted at all, which prompted him after an appreciable period to contact the school district, or he received a letter in the mail from different school districts. The statement Andy received, pursuant to both notices, was that Andy hadn't been successful for any of the position he applied for. Andy was shocked. He couldn't understand why he hadn't been successful given his impeccable and outstanding credentials. An ordinary candidate would just chalk the rejection up to bad luck, start searching again, and re-engage in the process. Andy, however, wasn't the ordinary candidate.

The more Andy thought about it, the less he could understand that he hadn't been offered a position. He had to make certain determinations. He needed to determine how far he wanted to take this issue. He determined that the decision rested on a few factors:

1. How did he do in the interviews?
2. Who was the successful candidate, and what were his or her credentials?
3. Was the successful candidate connected through a friend or relative of a power player in the district?
4. Was the successful candidate a member of a group? (race, religion, ethnicity, and so forth)?

Andy did the right thing by immediately requesting an after-action interview. An unsuccessful candidate should always contact the interviewers to inquire as to what discrepancies existed in his or her candidacy that required a failure. Andy asked whether he could come in and interview the interviewers regarding the interviews, including its failures and/or discrepancies and how it could be made better. Sometimes interviewers will agree to a telephone interview. Sometimes they will agree to a face-to-face interview. Andy wasn't so fortunate; not only did the interviewers not agree to a post-interview interview, but most didn't even take his call. At this time, Andy, believing he was an exemplary candidate and that some hanky-panky or underhanded activities had occurred in the application, interview, and/or hiring practice, decided to take the matter further.

Andy didn't get an opportunity to talk to the interviewers after the interviews, so he wrote a letter to the school districts that had refused to take his calls, indicating his concern about not obtaining the position. He indicated in the letter that he respectfully requested a post-interview interview but heard nothing. He then wrote another letter, in which he included a written "interview." Andy gave the interviewers the opportunity to answer certain questions, such as the following:

1. Was my demeanor appropriate for the interview?
2. Were my credentials appropriate for the position?
3. What made the successful candidate's candidacy superior to mine?
4. Is the successful candidate currently related to anyone in the district?
5. What is the racial and ethnic makeup of your school district as related to the following?
    a. African Americans
    b. Hispanics
    c. Women
    d. Men

Andy felt the questions were appropriate, but you get the point. The bottom line was that the interviewer realized Andy didn't believe it had necessarily been an objective or fair interview. Andy didn't receive any response from this letter, but it put the interviewer on notice that Andy didn't take the rejection lightly; at the very least, he or she would be on notice that the tenor of the interview was being called into question.

After Andy sent out that letter and received no responses, he followed up to ascertain who had been offered and received the position. This was a matter of public record. The opening itself was a matter of public record, and when the position was filled, it would have been noted in the board of education's meeting agenda and minutes.

If you are in this situation, here are some facts to remember. The minutes are a verbatim record of all the business the board conducted during the previous month. There is a board meeting once a month. Once you read the minutes of the board of education and ascertain who was hired for the position, you must ascertain all the information you can about that person. This won't be difficult since the person's degree, starting salary, and other information will be in the board minutes. Once you have the name of the person hired, you can inquire through the Open Public Records Act or similar legislation into the other credentials of this person.

You may be asking yourself, "Why would I go through all this trouble?" Of course, the answer to this query is whether you believe you were treated fairly during the application and interview process. If you don't believe you were, you might want to do some further research into the situation. For example, as was the case with Andy, if you determine that your credentials, being exemplary, were of record but that the person who was hired for the position had woefully inferior credentials compared to yours, you might wish to make further inquiry and ascertain whether something else was at work in the hiring or promotion practice. If you are a minority and the chosen applicant isn't and had credentials not even remotely as auspicious as yours, you might want to bring this fact to the attention of the interviewer and indicate that you will make further inquiries.

We can now assume that Andy took all the advice and suggestions herein provided and was able to secure a teaching position in a public school. His problems are over. Right? Wrong! Now that he has his first teaching position, he must keep it. The first three years of his teaching career are his most problematic. He can easily find himself unemployed after the first year and would ordinarily be powerless to prevent it.

The final part of the introduction to the profession of pedagogy as relates to the initial employment opportunity involves the keeping of the teaching position once it is secured. Teaching and other jobs in the public schools that require a certificate have a unique characteristic that exists in no other profession. That is that the certificated professional in public education (teacher, supervisor, vice/ assistant principal, principal, assistant superintendent, superintendent) must serve in an initial, probationary status before the professional obtains job security. In the profession of pedagogy, this job security is referred to as tenure. In most cases, tenure is obtained at the end of the first day of school in the beginning of the fourth year. The new teacher is, therefore, completely vulnerable for the first three years of service.

This issue is relevant because the obtaining of the initial employment in education is not the end of the issue, but the beginning. In other words, a non-tenured teacher has virtually no job security and runs the risk of being non-renewed at the conclusion of the teacher's annual employment contract. The new teacher must be offered and accept a new contract for the following school year at the end of the present school year. Once tenure is obtained, job security is secured and the teacher is relieved of the yearly obligation of securing a new contract, having secured a property right in his or her job. As a property right, the position cannot be taken away without due process of law.

In the world of school law, a "non-renewal" is distinct from a "discharge," "firing," or "termination". The latter usually occurs upon notice, and, in the public-school context, almost always for cause. A "non-renewal," however, can be with or without cause and can be promulgated for any or no reason.

In most school districts, the non-tenured teacher is provided a written notice as to whether he or she will be renewed or not for the next succeeding school year. If a teacher is non-renewed, he or she is usually afforded the opportunity to request a written statement of reasons for non-renewal and the ability to provide a written statement of reasons as to why he or she should be renewed.

He or she is usually afforded the opportunity to appear before the Board of Education to attempt to convince the Board to offer reemployment notwithstanding the Superintendent's failure to recommend renewal. State Commissioners of Education have constantly asserted that a non-tenured teacher can be non-renewed for any reason or no reason at all, so long as it is not a reason that would be "arbitrary, capricious, or unreasonable," such as, for example, discrimination or unlawful retaliation. This is where your limited power lies in the event of non-renewal.

My advice to non-tenured teachers is to involve yourself in nothing except your profession. If you have an opinion as to the curriculum, the assessments, the leadership style of your principal, the quality of food in the cafeteria, or anything else, KEEP IT TO YOURSELF! Concentrate on not only being an outstanding teacher, who comes in early and leaves late, but also who volunteers to chaperone the school dance and who volunteers to coach the volleyball team. At the faculty meetings when a volunteer is sought, your hand should fly up every time the word volunteer is spoken. Be ready willing and able not only to assist whenever necessary, but to let everyone know you are ready, willing, and able to do so.

If you are non-renewed, the people who know of your proclivity for volunteerism will usually be available to you for testimony before the board as to your good works. Of course, nothing, not even volunteerism will excuse poor performance and inefficiency in the classroom. The classroom is where you must shine. After you obtain tenure, you have more of an ability to safely pass upon aspects of the learning environment that are of concern to you.

The situation regarding promotions in the school districts, as opposed to hiring, is a little different. Usually, an unwritten rule and/or practice in the school districts is that the powers that be will usually identify the person favored to obtain the elevated position. Sometimes, the "favored one" is so obvious that everyone in the district knows who this person is. The principals, directors, supervisors, assistant superintendents, and superintendents have their favorites in the district. The persons earmarked for these elevated positions are those who have done substantial service to the district or for certain people in the district. That person may be favored because of some relationship he or she has with the powers that be in the district. That person might be related to the superintendent, assistant superintendent, city council member, or some other substantial individual in the community.

This leads us to the story of Amy Ambitious. Amy, a Hispanic vice principal of a middle school, wanted to become a school principal. She applied several times for a principalship, but individuals whose credentials were inferior to hers were usually the successful candidates. In the first year of the tenure of a recently appointed superintendent, she applied for three principalships. The first was for the principalship of an elementary school. The superintendent of schools awarded that principalship to a woman that the superintendent mentored, was friends with, and had helped obtain her advanced degrees.

Amy believed she had greater credentials than that person. Her credentials at the time consisted of several university degrees. The successful candidate possessed a bachelor's degree and a master's degree. Amy believed favoritism was at work in that situation.

That year Amy had two additional interviews but was denied. One was for a middle-school position. It was filled by the previous occupant of that position, whom the previous superintendent had transferred to an elementary school because of the school's poor performance. Amy knew he was more qualified than she since he had previously served as principal of that school, and that bias had nothing to do with that appointment. His movement created a principalship filled by a reading coach. She was a principal in another district and went on maternity leave from there and never returned. Amy had friends in that principal's old district who told her that this principal's previous district had advised her not to return.

Later, two additional elementary school principalships opened. One of the two candidates was an African American female, so Amy discounted that racism was at hand in the promotion process. The successful candidate was the protégé of a long-time, well-placed employee of the district. Amy thought her credentials were as good as those of the successful candidate. The second position was filled by a Caucasian woman, whose credentials paled in comparison to Amy's. After that denial, Amy put the superintendent of schools on notice that she thought the promotion practice was unfair.

Amy contacted the superintendent of schools and provided a factual delineation of her allegations. She spelled out what she thought the problem was, indicated her proof, and said what she believed was the result of the superintendent's actions. In her notice to the superintendent, Amy was careful not to mention in the written notice, that she thought the promotion practices of the district in might have been discriminatory. She did not want to provide any insight into her position before the actual meeting.

Be very careful about the correspondence you put in writing to the superiors you wish to address regarding any slight you feel you have suffered. You may not want to tip your hand to the individual to whom you wish to express concerns. Of course, given the nature of the situation, it may be appropriate to lay it out fully in your address to the superior. The approach you take depends on the situation and what advantage you believe you have in either approach. The superintendent contacted Amy to set up an interview in her office. That was when Amy indicated that she believed the promotion practices were discriminatory.

The superintendent was very gracious in the interview. This is a common tactic designed to disarm the complainant. Amy stuck to her guns, as you must. Amy told her straight out that she thought the superintendent's promotion practices were unfair. The superintendent dismissed the allegation out of hand. She indicated that nothing could be further from the truth. She indicated that she had promoted others based on fairness and equity and that as soon as she had become superintendent, she had sent around to all the staff and faculty members her policy regarding hiring and promotion.

Amy went over with her each promotion she felt she had been unfairly denied. She also indicated why she should have been chosen and why the candidate chosen had been inferior to her candidacy. The superintendent provided justifications for each promotion, the first more flimsy than the next, but none justified her actions. Amy got the impression that the superintendent was suggesting that she seek employment in other districts. That comment propelled Amy to file a complaint with the Equal Employment Opportunities Commission (EEOC) and the Attorney General's office, Division on Civil Rights.

I remind you that any action you promulgate against the school district and the superintendent is fraught with peril. You will be subject to retaliation, as Amy was. As a result of the complaint, the district made life difficult for Amy. She was transferred, given significantly more difficult assignments, and provided with inferior office space, equipment and provisions.

The Equal Employment Opportunity Commission (EEOC) reviewed Amy's case. The EEOC, after a review of a case, can do one of the following:

1. Find that the alleged facts fail to rise to a violation under the statute.
2. Adopt the findings of the state or local fair employment practices agency that investigated the charge, or,
3. Find that it is unable to conclude one way or the other that the information obtained establishes the violation of the statute. This is what happened in Amy's case.

If the EEOC finds that it is unable to decide, the claimant is free to file a suit on his or her own. Amy chose not to file a suit at that time. The important thing to remember is that you must be prepared for the long haul. You must be prepared to create a record.

Amy knew the possibility of success in the initial filing was a long shot. When the EEOC denied Amy's claim, she went to work. This was when her work in the case truly began.

The initial denial of your claim should spur you to action, whether it is a claim filed with the federal government, state, or your employer's grievance procedure.

You must be prepared to revisit this issue and continue to apply when openings occur. Every denial creates a new opportunity to create a record. Diligence and proof are the hallmarks of a good and successful action against a school district or any employer. Also, the district has a business administrator who will compile and amass documentation, lawyers who will pass on legal issues, and a slew of personnel who will do its bidding. All you have is yourself and whomever you might enlist to help you. Try to go to your collective bargaining unit to see whether it will provide legal support for your position. At least ask if it will refer this matter to its attorney for help. Amy had legal training and consequently had advantages; she had colleagues to help and her own legal research skills. You must attempt to obtain support, but ultimately you will need to be your most strident advocate.

Amy immediately began amassing documentation, records, and anything else she could get to establish the backgrounds of everyone who had interviewed for any of the positions she had sought. Amy was especially interested in the credentials of those who had been promoted. She consulted with a colleague and, pursuant to the Open Public Records Act, confronted the school district and demanded documentation pertinent to interviews for principal for a certain period.

The district complied and provided some of the documentation Amy had requested. Her colleague and she then arranged to meet to discuss the documentation received and whatever course of action they intended to pursue thereafter. After a review of the documentation provided and the theory developed involving the practice and attitude of the district regarding hiring and promotion practices, they concluded that certain documents hadn't been provided, and another demand letter was advanced. When the district attempted to ignore their requests for documentation, they turned up the volume and threatened litigation if the district didn't comply.

Thereafter, Amy obtained documentation regarding the hiring and promotion practices of the school district. Amy read district policies, superintendent policies, résumés, and various other documents. She spoke to many other disappointed promotion candidates and was able to track down some initial teaching candidates who had been denied employment. Amy was very expansive in her interviews of these people. She asked them questions such as the following:

1. What position did you apply for?
2. Do you remember who was on your interview committee?
3. How long did the interview last?
4. What questions were you asked?
5. Did you send a thank-you email or regular mail afterward?
6. How did you feel after you finished the interview?
7. Do you think you were treated fairly?

The information received from the documentation and the interviews Amy had with the unsuccessful candidates revealed much.

The district refused to provide Amy with a delineation of its working policy or its deliberations regarding the successful candidates. It indicated that providing these documents was an exception to the Open Public Records Act. Amy wasn't concerned, however, because she noticed a pattern regarding the hiring and promotion practices of the district. She noticed, for example, that candidates who were either related to a "heavy hitter" in the district or very close to someone there had very short interviews.

Amy had it on very good authority that the district would in the following year be inundated with several principal vacancies. Armed with this information, she developed a plan of action to use when the vacancies arose. She then allowed her paperwork and research to remain idle until the vacancies began to materialize.

The great takeaway of this chapter is to do your research and obtain documentation.

3

LOCAL GRIEVANCE PROCEDURES, THE EQUAL EMPLOYMENT OPPORTUNITIES COMMISSION (EEOC), AND THE DIVISION ON CIVIL RIGHTS (DCR)

The central consideration that prevails over all others is that the quest for fairness and equity isn't usually achieved after only one battle. Therefore, you must consider every defeat to be evidence of a continuing pattern by the district. You must continue to document, review, ask questions, obtain information, and analyze the district's continuing actions. You must also be prepared to fight in different forums.

Let us continue Amy's story. Later, five principal vacancies occurred: a high school, a middle school, and three elementary schools. Amy applied for each and was denied. Upper-echelon administrators in the district had friends, acquaintances, and relatives among the candidates. Discrimination was only a marginal issue there, but it was present in some circumstances. The predominant issue was blatant favoritism and bias. This reality is just as insidious as race or gender discrimination and must be called out when revealed.

The successful candidate for the middle school position was the principal of an elementary school. He was chosen over Amy, even though Amy was the vice principal of the school for which the principal vacancy existed. To bring someone into a school to lead the school who had no knowledge of the school—its students, faculty, staff, program, or parents—over Amy who had been an administrator in the school for a year seemed to indicate an issue of favoritism and bias. The successful candidate had been previously supervised by the principal of Amy's school. In other words, the principal of the school where Amy was vice principal was the former supervisor of the successful candidate. In the face of these blatantly biased and unfair practices, Amy filed a grievance with the district's affirmative action officer.

Amy filed with the district's affirmative action office those cases in which she thought racial discrimination was the reason for the denial. Although not necessary, as was the case when Amy previously filed with the EEOC, the initial arena in which an action alleging racial discrimination is usually filed is with the employer's affirmative action office. This will be in the form of a grievance. Most states require each school district to have an affirmative action officer. By statute, the affirmative action officer is usually obligated to investigate all allegations of discrimination.

The grievance is a document that requires significant care in drafting. Certain elements must be included in it. Amy included all these in her filing. The first and most important detail is that it must be dated within the period required for a grievance to be timely filed. If not, the affirmative action officer and/or the employer can dismiss the grievance on that ground alone. The second detail is that the grievance must be addressed to the district affirmative action officer. That officer must be named as the recipient of the written grievance. Immediately after naming the affirmative action officer, Amy was sure to designate the title "affirmative action officer."

The next item that must be contained in the grievance, arguably the most important, is the first sentence of the body. That sentence must not only state you are filing a grievance against the employer but also indicate the authority being cited to support your allegation of discrimination. Amy's initial sentence cited Title 7 of the Civil Rights Act of 1964, her local state statutes prohibiting discrimination, and her board of education's own affirmative action policy.

The next items that should be alleged in your grievance are the acts you cite that amount to the employer's improper conduct that rose to the level of discrimination. Immediately after Amy fulfilled the previously stated requirements, she indicated the acts she believed qualified as acts of discrimination. In this area, you should be as specific as possible regarding the act or acts you believe establish racial, gender, age, or whatever discrimination you allege. As a general statement of her belief in the practice by the school district of racial discrimination, Amy asserted "that certain high-level administrators have undertaken and engaged in promotion policies and practices that have discriminated against minorities; have favored their friends, associates, and mentees and their friends and relatives; and have sought to promote based not on background qualifications and seniority but on completely subjective standards hereinbefore delineated." As specific statements of her belief in the practices, she laid out:

1. The open position (principal)
    a. Where and when it was posted
2. The qualifications necessary for acquisition of the position
    a. Certificate, experience, etc.

3. Necessary submissions for application
   a. Cover letter, copy of certificate, resume

Next, she indicated that she was qualified for the position, applied for it, did not receive it, indicated information regarding the successful candidate. She then indicated the specific facts that she contended was the basis of her allegation of discrimination.

Most grievances must be initially submitted to the district through the collective bargaining unit the employee belongs to. This doesn't mean the collective bargaining unit, be it the education association most teachers and other employees belong to or the administrators' and supervisors' association most principals, vice principals, directors, and supervisors belong to, must take up the issue and submit the grievance to the school board in its name. Possibly, the collective bargaining unit might reject the grievance. If it does so, the employee is free to directly file the grievance with the affirmative action office against the school board.

In Amy's grievance, she wanted there to be no doubt as to her allegations, the facts, the case law she was relying on, how she had been harmed, what damages she was seeking, and how she intended to prove her case.

The last part of the grievance that is of significance is the last page. After you have concluded your grievance letter, you must print your name. The next entry is very important. You will recall that this letter of grievance was addressed to the affirmative action officer of the school district against whom you are filing the grievance. In my opinion, you must also send a copy of this grievance to the president of the board of education and the superintendent of schools. They are both significant players in this situation. By copying them on this letter, you not only notify them of what you are doing but also thereby expedite a resolution of this matter.

Once you have served the notice of grievance on the affirmative action officer and copied the president of the board of education, the only thing you can do is wait for a response. The response will usually be in the form of a letter from the affirmative action officer, which indicates he or she has received your notice of grievance and that it is going to be investigated pursuant to law and policy. In Amy's case, the situation was most unusual.

The affirmative action officer to whom Amy submitted her notice of grievance wrote her back, indicating that he couldn't investigate Amy's matter. He informed Amy that, because he sat on several of the interview committees Amy had appeared before, and because those very committees had denied her, he was conflicted and couldn't undertake an objective investigation into Amy's allegations. As an aside, it is patently insulting to realize that any school district could be so haphazard and cavalier regarding its hiring and promotion practices that it would place the affirmative action officer on an interview committee. It seems that even an idiot would be able to conclude and foresee the potential problem with such an appointment.

The conflict of interest cited by the affirmative action officer did not relieve the district of its obligation to investigate the matter. The district appointed its own legal counsel to undertake the investigation the law required it to undertake. Amy realized that it might be paranoia to attribute an underhanded motive to the district in creating a scenario in which the affirmative action officer was conflicted. She nevertheless recognized the significant benefit to the district in having its own, paid legal team to undertake a "fair and objective" investigation against its own employer.

Because of such, did the district intend to have any such allegations investigated by its own attorney to obtain a favorable disposition? These are certainly thoughts and possibilities. Here is a piece of advice to an employer who might read this book: If your intention is fairness and equity, *never* put an affirmative action officer on an interview committee.

Immediately after the affirmative action officer contacted Amy and indicated that he wouldn't be able to investigate Amy's grievance, the district's law firm contacted her. The purpose of the contact was to arrange an interview with Amy regarding her grievance. Amy determined that the firm had a significant conflict of interest and declined to participate in the investigation.

After Amy declined to participate in the investigation, the law firm contacted her again. It indicated that it had contacted her and sought to set up an interview regarding the grievance. Through its representative, the law firm indicated that no investigation could be undertaken without the grievant providing a statement to initiate the investigation. It also acknowledged Amy's concurrent refiling against the district with the Equal Employment Opportunity Commission (EEOC) and the local civil rights division of the attorney general's office.

When someone attempts to confront a significant entity with legal action, he or she can expect the entity to retaliate with significant force. Perhaps it was instinct or Amy's legal training that indicated to her that the district was engaged in underhanded and improper conduct either in the actions that compelled the recusal of the affirmative action officer or in its insistence that Amy be interviewed before the law firm could undertake an investigation. Amy's opinion was that the way the law was written indicated that no matter whether the grievant was interviewed, once a grievance was filed, alleging discrimination against a school district, an investigation had to commence. She indicated this position to the law firm, but it disagreed.

The filing of the new action with the EEOC and the local civil rights division was intended as an offset to the nefarious conduct of the school district. More and more, Amy came to believe that the cards were stacked against her in this matter. She believed that either the district's law firm would refuse to investigate the case on the ground that she had refused to cooperate by being interviewed or that it would find in favor of the district, its employer, no matter what the investigation revealed. Amy, therefore, also contacted the state's department of education. Believing that she wouldn't be able to get a fair investigation by the district's own law firm, she petitioned the commissioner of education to investigate her grievance.

The quest for justice is sometimes a learning experience. We all seek justice, but we don't always know how to obtain it. Even with her legal training, Amy wasn't sure of the appropriate actions she could take to redress the grievances she had against the school district. Amy filed a petition with the commissioner of education, requesting that it investigate the allegations Amy had advanced in her filings with the EEOC and the local affirmative action office and with the Division of Civil Rights of the Attorney General's office. Having researched the issue and having been advised that the commissioner's office didn't undertake such investigations, Amy amended her petition to request that the commissioner appoint an independent organization to undertake the investigation.

The commissioner's office declined to either undertake an investigation of the district itself or appoint an independent agency to engage in such. The representative did indicate that she could petition to determine the propriety of having a school district investigate an allegation of discrimination against it by its own attorney. Amy was advised that the conflict-of-interest issue could be adjudicated through the Administrative Office of the Courts.

After she contacted the Office of Controversies and Disputes in the Department of Education, she filed a petition in which she alleged that the procedure of the school district in allowing its board attorney to impartially investigate her allegations of racial discrimination and bias was inappropriate. The commissioner acknowledged the filing of Amy's petition. He or she also acknowledged the answer provided by the school district's law firm. Finally, Amy received a notice from the Office of Administrative Law acknowledging the filing of her action with it. This was a significant notice since the matter was now rightfully in the hands of the courts.

On many occasions, a petitioner in the filing of a case like this can't afford or is otherwise disinclined to hire an attorney. The procedure in many actions of this type allows non-lawyers to represent litigants. That is very significant because Amy was a pro se litigant. That simply means she represented herself in this matter. She felt comfortable doing so because she had legal training and was conversant with the filing of pleadings and the receipt of answers from adversaries. Not everyone is comfortable taking this step on his or her own. If you feel comfortable with a union representative, a knowledgeable friend, or someone else who has experience in these matters, that person might be able to represent you in a matter like this, even though that person is not an attorney at law.

When a petition is filed, the person against whom the petition is advanced must answer it. The school board answered through its attorney. It was merely a handful of denials.

4

THE CONSOLIDATION OF MULTIPLE FILINGS

My suggestion to any applicant or employee who believes he or she has been wrongfully passed over for employment or denied promotion based on race or other factors recognized by recent Supreme Court holdings as "suspect categories"[3] is to file actions in as many forums as possible. This is what Amy did. This step is good for many reasons: it gives the employer notice that you are serious, you have many more chances of obtaining a favorable result, you have a better ability to understand how your adversary (the employer) will respond, and the extended work involved for your adversary might encourage a settlement.

Your adversary, however, doesn't want you to file the same action in different forums. The reason is obvious: it's too much work for which he or she must respond and respond he or she must. Ignoring any allegation

---

[3] A presumptively unconstitutional distinction made between individuals on the basis of race, national origin, alienage, or religious affiliation. Korematsu v. U.S., 323 U.S. 214 (1944)

of this kind is not only illegal but also unethical and would ultimately be a public relations nightmare for the district. Your adversary would rather answer only once. If, however, you file with the Equal Employment Opportunity Commission (EEOC), the state division on civil rights, and the school district's affirmative action division, the employer must engage with all three of these separate entities and answer each petition. If the school district failed to answer in any of the entities in which you filed an action, the failure might be deemed as an admission of your contentions.

The school district against whom Amy filed her petitions attempted to consolidate her actions. In other words, the school district attempted to combine two separate causes of action into one. Amy filed with the commissioner of education and with the division on civil rights of the state attorney general's office. The facts were identical in both cases. The administrative code provides for consolidation where similar or identical facts exist in two contiguously filed cases. Those in the school district wanted consolidation because they didn't want to have to answer two separate cases alleging the same facts. Amy didn't want a consolidation because she wanted to know how the school made its decisions regarding its promotion practices. This information would have been provided to Amy by a device called "discovery." The school district would have had to file two separate answers and engage in two separate sets of discovery practices. It is now appropriate to explain the rudiments of civil procedure.

All civil cases start with a pleading. The complaint is a pleading, filed by the plaintiff that starts the case. The answer by the defendant usually ends the pleadings phase of the case. There are several other pleadings, such as a cross-claim, a counterclaim and a third-party claim, but our purposes only require knowledge of the complaint and the answer. The discovery process in legal jurisprudence commences when the pleading phase ends and is as important as the pleading phase. This phase involves each side exchanging information it intends to use to support its position. The information could be documents, laboratory results, or statements. Almost any documentation pertinent to that side's position in the case is included in the discovery.

Discovery practice is an art in and of itself. It is a crucial aspect of any case filed in court. A form of discovery is also used in nonjudicial and quasi-judicial practice. It is always in the best interest of the parties to obtain an idea of the strength and quality of the other side's case. Discovery is very ancient and widely encouraged as having the ability to resolve issues short of a trial. It is also crucial regarding motion practice and settlement procedures. The timing and sequence of discovery is also important.

The first aspect of discovery is usually the propounding of interrogatories to the adversary. Interrogatories are merely a set of questions in written form that are submitted to the adversary. These questions must be answered. If the person or party to whom the questions were given doesn't believe the questions were answered truthfully, accurately, or completely, the aggrieved party is free to go to court and make a motion for more specifics regarding the response to the interrogatories. The interrogatories are used to proceed to the next major step in the discovery process, which is taking depositions.

Depositions are usually but not always generated by the information contained in the response to interrogatories. This is the process whereby some person who might have information regarding the case could be required to attend a session by way of the submission of a subpoena[4]

---

[4] Ballantine, James A., and William S. Anderson, 1969, Ballantine's Law Dictionary, with pronunciations, Rochester, NY – Lawyer's Co-Operative Publishing Company.(The ordinary process by which the attendance of a witness in court (or other place), is compelled, being issued by the clerk of the Court.)

requiring the person to appear at some place, usually the lawyer's office. (*Subpoena* is Latin for "under pain.") If ignored, one will be "under pain" from the court for such a transgression inasmuch as the Court might impose a sanction for ignoring it. At that session, questions would be asked. It is almost like taking testimony in a trial, except there's no judge or courtroom. The stenographer is there, and every word stated in the deposition is taken down verbatim just like in a courtroom.

In Amy's case in the administrative law court, she requested discovery. The administrative law judge, however, denied her request. The judge held Amy's request in abeyance. In other words, the judge decided to put off ruling on the request because it was thought that the case could be resolved by way of summary judgment. Summary judgment is granted when the court concludes there is no real material issue of fact or law that requires proceeding to a full-blown trial. The court indicated that if after a hearing it concluded there were material issues of fact and/or law to be resolved, it could issue a discovery order then.

The school district's position was that there was a filing in two forums of a case with almost identical facts. It asserted that one of those forums was the appropriate place in which to bring the action. It asserted further that one of these entities, either the Department of Education or the attorney general's office, had an interest that was superior to the other entity's interest; therefore, it should be the one in whose forum the issue was resolved. Amy's position was that neither entity had a superior interest. Amy wanted to prosecute this matter in both forums so she could see the facts and documentation the district was going to rely on and how each entity would deal with them.

The matter was assigned to an administrative law judge. The judge initially scheduled a prehearing conference. A prehearing conference is a procedural step in most court cases intended to resolve technical issues. The time, place, and manner of the hearing are set as well as a resolution of any matters, such as the time of filing of briefs and other issues. Amy's hearing was to be done by telephone.

The conference was held. It was a telephonic phone conference with the judge on one phone, the lawyer for the school district on another phone, and Amy on her phone. A week or so later, the judge sent a letter to both Amy and her adversary, memorializing the content of the prehearing conference. This is a usual practice of judges after a hearing to avoid any misunderstanding of what occurred at the hearing, including what each side would be responsible for, when they would be responsible for it, and what the next procedure would be.

The letter from the judge indicated that Amy's adversary's motion to consolidate with predominant interest would be held in abeyance. She also indicated that Amy's request for discovery would be held in abeyance and that the next proceeding would be cross motions for a summary decision. She ordered that both sides submit briefs, in which each party's position would be laid out. Later, she indicated that briefs in this matter would be due soon and that oral argument would be held thereafter.

A brief is a concise statement of authorities in various forms suitable to the purpose of counsel or the court. It is an exposition of the procedural history, facts, law, issues, position of the party submitting it, and the conclusions to be drawn. It is designed, not only to provide the adversary with the position of the submitter of the item, but to acquaint the Court with the significant fundamentals of the dispute that exists between the parties.[5]

---

[5] Ballantine, James A., and William S. Anderson, 1969, Ballantine's Law Dictionary, with pronunciations, Rochester, NY – Lawyer's Co-Operative Publishing Company.

Even though the judge indicated that she would hold the issue of the motion of Amy's adversary to consolidate both matters and to determine the predominant interest in abeyance, Amy was proactive. As was stated, the judge narrowed the issue to be determined to whether the board action in referring Amy's affirmative action complaint to its attorneys for investigation was an appropriate exercise of the board's discretion or if it was an act that was arbitrary, capricious, and/or unreasonable.

It is imperative for you as an adversary to a powerful organization to understand that you must not be satisfied with providing the bare minimum. You are standing in the face of an entity that has almost unlimited funds, unlimited logistical support, and presumptive support in the community, namely the school board or other employment giant. This is an entity that has its basis of legitimacy in statute, code, local support, political support, and community support. The individuals who run the school board are usually elected officials. When they are not, the mayor who appoints them is an elected official. The mayor regularly intermingles with the community. It is a common inclination of anyone who deals regularly with such an entity (or elected official) to give the benefit of the doubt to such an entity (or elected official). This is the burden you face.

Amy submitted her brief on the issue of whether the board's action in referring her affirmative action complaint to its attorneys for investigation was an appropriate exercise of the board's discretion or was arbitrary, capricious, and/or unreasonable. She also submitted a brief on the issue of whether an independent body should investigate the school district. Amy submitted this brief to the court. The court in which an action is pending might order the parties to submit a brief, or summation of the facts and the law in the matter. Since she hadn't been ordered to do so, she wasn't required to submit a copy to her adversary. Amy thought the court should have an expanded insight into the practices of the school district. This is in line with the "extra" referred to earlier.

If you are a grievant levying a complaint against a school district or any employer, you must understand that it is a David-versus-Goliath situation. You are one lone person against a monolith. The organization against whom you complain has almost unlimited time, resources, finances, logistics, and momentum to defend against you. You have virtually none of those things. That is why you must concentrate on obtaining documentation from the employer on all aspects of its general hiring and promotion practices and those documents involved in and generated by your specific case. If discrimination exists, it will be found and proven by their own words as revealed in their documentation. As will be revealed later, this was the fact in Amy's case.

Your best bet to succeed in this kind of case is to acquire as much information and documentation possessed by your employer. The more documentation you obtain, the greater the possibility exists that you will find an inconsistency, contradiction, or implicit admission of impropriety in the practice and/or procedures of your employer's hiring and promotion practice. That is where your success lies.

Amy argued that the use of its attorney—in one case to advocate on behalf of the school district and on the other to provide an objective, neutral analysis of the same facts—was inherently a conflict of interest. She further argued that any court case she filed as a result of the findings and recommendations of the investigation would prevent her from obtaining the results of the investigation because the investigator would be the attorney of her adversary. The attorney could therefore argue "work product" and refuse to turn over the results of the investigation.

It is appropriate to discuss the doctrine of work product since it relates to discovery in civil litigation. The work product doctrine protects materials prepared by an attorney and/or anyone working for the attorney in anticipation of litigation.[6] This work product cannot, therefore, be demanded as discovery. You will recall that reference was made to the absolute necessity of obtaining as much information about the employer's promotion and hiring practices as possible to be successful in an action against the employer based on discrimination. This would consist of interrogatories, signed statements, and other information acquired for the prosecution or defense of any case.

The significant part of this issue for our purposes, namely for an attorney investigating a case who is also in another case representing the same adversary on the same facts, is that the attorney while conducting the investigation will document thoughts, conclusions, and impressions regarding the viability of the contentions raised by the grievant. These thoughts could be crucial to a case involving an issue as subjective as discrimination. However, mental impressions, conclusions, opinions, or legal theories of counsel are never discoverable by an opposing party. This was the core of Amy's argument at this point of her brief.

The attorney who acts both as an independent, objective investigator and as a biased, partial advocate on the same facts while representing the party against whom the investigation has been promulgated lends a significant advantage to his client. The attorney can simultaneously present information gleaned as part of the investigation to the finder of fact (the school board) and thereafter provide to his or her client (the school board) the possible meaning and import of these facts. The attorney can advance his or her theory of the case and his or her legal advice, none of which is discoverable by the grievant.

An illustration of the predicament envisioned in this contention is appropriate. If a school board is accused of discrimination and a grievant presses the issue by demanding an investigation, the school board

---

[6] Hickman v. Taylor, 329 U.S. 495 (1947)

refers the matter to its affirmative action officer for investigation. The affirmative action officer undertakes the investigation by interviewing witnesses, propounding interrogatories, and obtaining the answers to them, documenting actions of the school board's hiring and promotion practices, and amassing statistical data regarding rates of hiring of races and ethnicities and other actions.

The affirmative action officer concludes the investigation and turns over findings and recommendations to the school board. The finding is that there has been no discrimination practiced against the grievant. The recommendation is that no action be taken. The grievant, unsatisfied with the findings and recommendations, files suit against the school board in the superior court on the grounds of discrimination. The grievant is entitled through discovery to the information the investigator amassed during the investigation.

Here is the same scenario, but now we substitute the school board's attorney for the affirmative action officer. The attorney conducts the investigation and amasses the same information: significant documentation, statistical analysis, witness interviews, and so forth. Same result. Now when the grievant files suit in the superior court, the discovery phase of the action commences. The grievant cannot wait to get his or her hands on all the documentation amassed during the investigation. The attorney refuses to turn it over and doesn't allow the school board to turn over anything he or she provided as findings and recommendations on the grounds that all this information is work product of the attorney in anticipation of the grievant's lawsuit against his or her client.

If you intend to proceed with a grievance against your school board, retaining an attorney is a good idea. Most attorneys who hold themselves out to be employment attorneys take only those cases that are presumptively lucrative or are "slam dunk" cases. Amy approached seven or eight attorneys to prosecute her case. None were interested.

A consideration to be given as to whether you will retain an attorney is how you will pay the attorney. Many attorneys take cases on a contingent-fee basis. This simply means the attorney agrees to take the case and obtain a percentage of any monetary award. This, of course, depends on the successful conclusion of the case. This requires that the attorney believe that the case has merit, and that the prosecution of the case will be successful. Some attorneys, having doubts as to the possible success of the case but still willing to engage, will take the case on an hourly basis, having obtained a substantial retainer up front.

If the case were taken on a contingent-fee basis, the attorney would get about one-third of any award. If it were taken on an hourly basis with a retainer up front, that could really run into an expensive proposition, and in the end, you might wind up losing the case and be out thousands and thousands of dollars. It is therefore in your best interest to attempt at least some legal research on your own and do some investigation, legal research, and filing of papers yourself, at least initially. Every county has a law library. It is usually located in the courthouse. The law library is usually supervised by a full-time librarian, who could help you find document preparation manuals and other legal research resources. There are a few necessities before you arrive: be conversant with the facts of your case and be aware of a few fundamentals.

Another aspect you should consider regarding your grievance involves the use of precedent to establish your case Precedent is an aspect of law that is technical in nature and primarily of interest to attorneys and judges. The American legal system relies on precedent to establish its core of operation. This simply means an attorney can usually predict how a court will rule in a certain case based on how another court of higher jurisdiction ruled in a set of the same or similar facts. A grievant shouldn't be shy about attempting to assert claims as a pro se litigant as Amy did. *Pro se* is a Latin term that indicates the litigant is prosecuting or defending an action on his or her own without the benefit of counsel. Even though Amy had legal training, she was considered a *pro se* litigant.

When you go to the law library, ask the librarian to direct you to the law encyclopedias. The two most well-known and detailed are the *Corpus Juris Secundum* and *American Jurisprudence*. These references define terms and causes of action. You might want to look up "grievance," "employment discrimination," "affirmative action," and similar terms. It would also be a good idea to have the law librarian direct you to the state statute and codes that govern education, affirmative action requirements of school boards, and the requirement of school boards regarding grievance filings. You should also possess your local school board's collective bargaining agreement, which was entered into between your school board and your local collective bargaining unit. That document will spell out the procedure to be engaged in should you or anyone decide to file a grievance against the school board.

Once you are conversant with definitions, procedures, and statutory language, you should ask the law librarian to direct you to the "forms" periodicals. For now, just acquaint yourself with what a pleading looks like, what it contains, and how it is set up. Remember, in any action, be it a grievance, civil complaint, or any other filing in any forum, there is a time limit involved. Even if you aren't sure you have filed properly, you must be aware of the deadline for filing your grievance. If you are late in filing—in other words, if you have exceeded the statute of limitations—you are going to be out of luck.

5

THE ADMINISTRATIVE OFFICE OF THE COURTS, THE COMMISSIONER OF EDUCATION, AND THEIR ROLE IN GRIEVANCE PROCEDURES

After Amy submitted her briefs to the court, her adversaries submitted their briefs. Amy's adversary submitted a very detailed brief, in which it denied the legal sufficiency of Amy's contentions. The court largely accepted the attempt by her adversary to refute her contentions. Suffice it to say, Amy's adversary's brief was a detailed, legal document that had as its purpose the total denial of the district's wrongdoing. As indicated earlier, when you go up against a monolithic organization, you will have a very difficult objective ahead of you.

Once the briefs were submitted, oral arguments were held. Amy and her adversary appeared before a judge. The judge indicated that he had read their briefs. The judge congratulated them on the thoroughness and completeness of their briefs. The judge then entertained arguments from both sides. Since Amy was the petitioner, she went first.

If your tactic against your employer includes a filing in court, you will be expected to file a brief and engage in an oral argument. For Amy, her argument wasn't a big deal. She had legal training. Some say the oral argument is a waste of time. Those individuals opine that the judge had already made up his or her mind based on the briefs. These same individuals contend that the oral argument is merely an exercise engaged in because court rules allow it. Amy didn't agree. She thought the oral argument gave the litigant the opportunity to advocate his or her position. It allowed the advocate to stress certain aspects of the case that mere words on paper couldn't. Oral argument gives you the opportunity to highlight your brief. In Amy's case, she infused at every opportunity the absolute unfairness of the school district's practices. At every opportunity, Amy emphasized the favoritism, nepotism, and absolute discrimination the school district commonly practiced and why it would be a gross miscarriage of justice to allow the district's law firm to conduct this investigation.

Amy emphasized to the judge that when openings occurred, it wasn't at all a secret most of the time who would be selected. It was usually someone with a last name that was similar to the last name of someone already in the district or a well-known and well-placed individual in the district. During her oral argument, Amy also took the opportunity to indicate how long and varied the practice had been. She subtly infused the proposition that there had been a long-standing practice of reserving key positions for members of certain races to the exclusion of the members of other races. Her reference to this practice got so pervasive in her oral argument that her adversary objected and pointed out to the court that Amy was injecting into her argument allegations that hadn't been briefed and that the adversary hadn't had the opportunity to respond to in writing.

After Amy finished her argument, the court turned to her adversary. The judge asked Amy's adversary certain questions Amy had raised not only in her brief but also in her argument to the court. The judge seemed to be very interested in her argument regarding the work product referred to earlier. Amy got the impression that the judge found this to be the most interesting argument raised in her brief. He found it, according to his own words, to be a very interesting argument. He asked Amy's adversary something point-blank. If Amy wanted to seek redress of her grievances in court, would the law firm rely on work product to keep the result of the investigation from her after a motion for discovery? Amy's adversary denied that such an action would be taken.

After the court heard the arguments of counsel, it indicated that it would take the matter under advisement. That is a common practice of judges after oral argument. It is very rare for a judge to render a decision right then and there after an argument. Very soon thereafter, the judge issued a written finding and recommendation.

It is appropriate at this time to discuss the procedure undertaken in a case like this. Usually, when a court renders a decision in this type of case, the decision is reduced to an order and made part of the record of the case. It is then filed with the clerk of the court. Except for an appeal, the case is over.

This was an administrative court, however. This matter was referred to this court by the commissioner of the Department of Education. The judge's decision, therefore, was merely advisory to the commissioner. The commissioner could accept, reject, or modify the decision.

The court decided that the school board's decision to allow its law firm to conduct this investigation was perfectly proper. It ruled that there was no prohibition by statute, code, or case law that disallowed such. It indicated that Amy's reliance on certain cases was misplaced or inaccurate. Amy realized she had a high burden to overcome. To disallow the action of the school board in appointing its own attorney to conduct the investigation, Amy had to show that the action of the school board was arbitrary, capricious, or unreasonable. She thought nothing could be clearer than the inherent conflict of interest in a school board attorney who was at once a neutral investigator and at the same time an advocate on the same facts against the same party and on the payroll of what it was being asked to investigate.

As indicated, the judge's findings and recommendations were just that. Amy had one more card to play. She was able to submit an appeal directly to the commissioner of education.

Amy then filed exceptions to the findings and recommendation of the judge with the education commissioner. The premise of her exceptions to the findings and recommendations of the judge was that the judge too narrowly construed and interpreted the civil rights statutes. It is appropriate for an explanation of her meaning regarding the construction of statutes.

When the state legislatures or the Congress of the United States promulgates a statute, it is usually to be interpreted broadly or narrowly. It depends on the purpose of the statute and the results of the interpretation. Criminal statutes are always interpreted narrowly. That means no extraneous or inappropriate meaning is to be attributed to the plain language of the statute. It is not appropriate to interpret it to imply that it might mean something other than, or in addition to, what the plain language of the text says. This is to protect a defendant from being charged with and/or convicted of something the text of the statute doesn't specifically prohibit.

Civil rights statutes are just the opposite. These have traditionally been interpreted broadly. It has long been a "familiar canon of statutory construction that remedial legislation should be construed broadly to effectuate its purposes" *Tcherepnin v. Knight*, (389 U.S. 332) (1967)).

Civil rights statutes are "remedial statutes." In other words, they are promulgated to remedy or cure past ills. At one point in our history, discrimination was the rule and the norm. Its vestiges have wreaked havoc and destroyed the life, liberty, and prosperity of millions of people over multiple generations.

For these statutes to have any ability to eliminate the badges and vestiges of entrenched racism in our society, the statutes would have to be interpreted broadly. In other words, not only should the plain language of the statute be used to offset racism, but any inferential or implicit discrimination should be addressed by the statute. Only by an interpretation of this kind would the subtleties of racism in all its forms be addressed.

Amy argued to the commissioner that what had occurred to her was blatant discrimination on the part of the school district, that it had happened on more than one occasion, and that this was the usual practice of the district against not only her but also several professionals seeking different positions. Amy further argued that to allow the district to use its own paid advocates to advance an objective and neutral investigation into her allegations was only the latest device of the district to continue its nefarious practices of discrimination.

The judge's findings were essentially that, since neither code nor statute expressly prohibited the use of a school district's attorney to conduct an investigation in the face of the disqualification of its affirmative action officer to conduct the investigation, it was lawful. Amy's argument to the commissioner was that it was irrelevant that the law didn't expressly prohibit the conduct. If the conduct could be interpreted as having the ability to result in a discriminatory purpose and/or effect and if that effect was or arguably could be realized, then the broad interpretation of the civil rights laws in the code and the statute could work to disallow the practice.

Amy submitted additional, unrequested materials to the court for this reason. She wanted to show how the superintendent had for years used the promotion practice of the school district as her own favored, nepotistic, and discriminatory employment practice. Amy wanted to show that the superintendent's actions had gone unchecked and had been continuously rubber-stamped by the school board, which had clearly abdicated its role as the final arbiter of correctness and fairness in all actions related to the school district.

The standard of review, as previously indicated, was the arbitrariness, capriciousness, or unreasonableness of the district's actions. Amy thought the narrow interpretation established this.

Notwithstanding Amy's argument for the necessity of the antidiscrimination statute to prevail over all others and that the appointment of the school board's attorney to conduct a neutral and fair investigation, while at the same time representing the school board in a different forum on essentially the same facts, was arbitrary, capricious, and unreasonable, the commissioner found in favor of the school board. Amy's fight to keep the school board's attorney from conducting the investigation was over.

In your quest for fairness and equity, you will suffer many defeats. Rather than risk a refusal to investigate, Amy decided to cooperate with and allow the investigation. This battle was over. The war raged on. What Amy's adversary didn't realize was that it would provide many more opportunities for her to ultimately prevail.

6

THE NEW GRIEVANCE AND REPETITIVENESS OF THE DISTRICT'S DISCRIMINATORY ACTS

A ny school district or employer who engages in unequitable and/or discriminatory acts has an unfortunate tendency to repeat these acts. This could be attributed to ego, complacency, or any number of factors. It could also be attributed to many moving parts in the district making personnel decisions based on factors other than hiring and promoting the most qualified person for the job. This was Amy's school district's significant failing.

As indicated, the acts of favoritism and discrimination perpetrated against Amy predominated with the appointment of a certain superintendent. This superintendent was appointed after serving a term as assistant superintendent. Almost immediately after she was appointed, three openings for principal positions materialized. The following year, two principalships were created. The year after that, five principal positions became vacant. Amy applied for all these positions. In all, ten principal positions were available. For some of these positions,

Amy knew she wasn't the most qualified candidate. This was true of only two or maybe three of these positions.

Soon thereafter, two events occurred that were the watershed of Amy's actions against the school district. First, she obtained her Doctor of Education degree (EdD). Second, a principal position opened for an elementary school. This job application was to be Amy's quintessential test of the school district's promotion policy. She applied for this position. It was inconceivable to Amy that she wouldn't get it. After all, she applied for the position after she had obtained her doctorate, which represented her fourth university degree, including her second doctorate degree. The advertisement for the position indicated that only internal candidates would be considered. Amy knew no internal candidate; in other words, no one already working in the district even remotely possessed her credentials.

Not only did Amy not attain the position, but the person hired was a classroom teacher with no administrative experience. This person had only two university degrees, the highest one being a master's degree. It was apparent to Amy that the district once again openly and blatantly practiced discrimination and didn't care that its actions were obvious. The successful candidate was a Caucasian female, a favorite of the previous principal, whom she and Amy had both worked for. She was a teacher in the school where Amy was the vice principal. Amy also knew the principal had put in several very good words to the superintendent about the candidacy of this person. Amy filed another grievance.

As a matter of protocol and procedure, it is imperative that you be aware of an additional factor. This requirement is as important as the filing of your grievances and other actions. I refer to the collective bargaining agreement between your educational association or other collective bargaining unit and the school board. It is critical that you acquaint yourself with the grievance procedures of the school district.

These procedures are in this agreement. As indicated earlier, the school district has a battery of lawyers it retains. The school district has virtually unlimited resources and logistical help. It can contact its lawyers anytime for any issue. It will not hesitate to do so when an annoying individual like Amy deigns to confront it with allegations of its impropriety.

The collective bargaining agreement in existence at the time Amy filed her second grievance with the school board required that she submit notice of the grievance to her immediate supervisor. That was the principal of the school where Amy served as vice principal. He notified Amy in writing that he wasn't empowered to grant the relief she sought. The grievance would then be forwarded to the next echelon of authority.

The notice by Amy's immediate supervisor prompted her to follow the grievance procedures and notify the next levels, namely the assistant superintendent of schools and then the superintendent of schools. The superintendent of schools, by correspondence to the president of her collective bargaining unit, quite surprisingly provided a written defense of Amy's allegations.

The school board attorney undoubtedly advised the superintendent of schools to allow any responses from the school district to come from the board attorneys. This would have been the best practice. Nevertheless, the superintendent felt the need to respond to Amy's allegations in her own voice.

This circumstance is quite interesting and deserves some review. Amy initially raised the issue of the racism and favoritism of the superintendent of schools, two years before. Two years later, the superintendent decided to respond to Amy's allegations of racism. The superintendent had been silent for more than two years regarding Amy's allegations. The superintendent chose to respond to the allegations by use of statistical data to support her contention that her hiring and promotion practices were fair.

Why do you suppose she did this? She did so because of the relentless and pervasive nature of Amy's allegations. This is a lesson for you. As previously indicated and in a continuous theme throughout this book, you must be prepared to prosecute your case for the long haul. The school board is going to rely on your unwillingness or inability to go all the way with your allegations. It will count on your fear of it. It will be comforted by the fact that in your quest for legal representation, most attorneys won't take this kind of case. It knows that it has the upper hand in such a matter.

The stronger and more relentless you are, the more you believe in the rightness of your position, and the more energy you are willing to expend, the greater the possibility of success. The superintendent responded like he did because he was feeling the heat. To quote an old maxim, if you say something enough times and loudly enough to enough people, it starts to look true no matter if it is or not. Amy had the benefit of her contentions being true, and silence didn't help the superintendent's position.

In her response to Amy's allegations of discrimination, the superintendent of schools provided the president of Amy's collective bargaining unit an in-depth analysis of her hiring and promotion practices as they related to race and gender issues. She provided information regarding the race and gender of his most recent promotions. She provided a statistical analysis of the hiring and promotion practices related to the race of the past three superintendents. Amy thought this act on the part of the superintendent was evidence of her abject racism. Had she been truly innocent of the charges and merely misunderstood, she would have remained silent and let her attorney respond. Amy knew from her experience in law that the one who shouted his or her innocence the loudest was usually guilty.

Amy read the superintendent's defense of her allegations from Amy with great interest. Amy found it necessary to respond to her defense and provided it to the president of her collective bargaining unit. Amy pointed out how disingenuous the superintendent of schools had been in her defense. Some of the things the superintendent had alleged were true. She had failed in most instances, however, to provide context for her statement. For example, she said she had promoted an African American to the principalship of the middle school. She failed to point out that the person she had made principal of the middle school was already a principal in the district. She had just moved that person to a new school with a new pay grade. The title was still "principal"; the promotion was in salary only, not in dignity, prestige, or responsibility within the district.

She also referred to her "promotion" of an African American to the principalship of an elementary school. She failed to point out, however, that this person was the significant professional partner and mentee of the person who would ultimately become assistant superintendent of schools. This fact lent significant credibility to Amy's assertion of favoritism in the district. The person to whom the superintendent referred was a vice principal of a school the soon-to-be-appointed assistant superintendent was principal of. This person was very close to the superintendent of schools, and an opinion regarding promotions and individuals who should be considered for positions by this person was formidable.

All previous filings and notices to subordinate authorities had failed; therefore, to formalize and finalize the pleadings in her grievance against the board, Amy, pursuant to the grievance procedures, contacted the board of education. She sent a letter to the president advising that she demanded a hearing before the board for a determination of her grievance. The step after the board's determination was nonbinding arbitration, which was worthless.

As indicated earlier, to achieve the justice you deserve in hiring and promotions, you must be relentless. Every time your school district posts another vacancy, you must apply for it. If you have already filed a grievance because of a failure in a previous application and you apply for a new opening and are unsuccessful, that is a new grievance. The exception, of course, is whether the successful candidate was in a protected or suspect status or class.

It is imperative that you understand what is actionable regarding hiring and promotion practices. The Supreme Court has identified certain protected statuses or classes. These are members of groups who have historically been discriminated against; if they are denied a hire or promotion, certain legal suspicions will arise as to the reason for denial of that person's candidacy. Applicants, employees, and former employees are protected from employment discrimination based on race, color, religion, sex (including pregnancy, sexual orientation, or gender identity), national origin, age (forty or older), disability, and genetic information (including family medical history).

Amy filed her first grievance as a result of being passed over for promotion for each of the five principalships she had applied for. Thereafter, an elementary school principalship opening occurred immediately after Amy obtained her doctorate in education. Not only was Amy unsuccessful, but the successful candidate wasn't in a protected status; nor did he have one doctorate degree, whereas Amy had two. He had never been an administrator, but at the time of her application, Amy had been a vice principal for eight years, and generally she was a better candidate. Amy filed another grievance.

Amy had refused to cooperate in the first proposed investigation on the grounds that it was invested with a conflict of interest. The law firm initially refused to undertake the investigation because Amy refused to cooperate on the grounds of a conflict of interest. By the time Amy filed her second grievance, the court and the commissioner had determined that the district's law firm was free to conduct the investigation.

You should understand that the law firm's position was that if Amy didn't cooperate with it in the undertaking of the investigation of her grievance (or either of them), it was under no obligation to conduct an investigation. Amy didn't believe that was true. She knew that neither the code nor the statute required any cooperation or even any input from the grievant, but what mandated an investigation by the school district was the receipt of a grievance.

The district's law firm didn't hesitate to point out to Amy that it didn't believe it was under any obligation to conduct any investigation she didn't cooperate with. It acknowledged in correspondence to Amy that she was unsuccessful in her petition before the administrative law court and in her appeal to the commissioner of education on the issue of the inappropriateness of the district's law firm in conducting the investigation. In the same correspondence, it acknowledged both of Amy's grievances and indicated its willingness to conduct the investigation should Amy decide to cooperate with it.

At some point, you must make a cost-benefit analysis of your actions. Amy could have insisted that the investigation go forward and have the district refuse. Amy would then have had to go back to court for a ruling regarding that issue. Amy concluded that enough time had been expended in litigation. She concluded that if she should decide to go to court on the merits of the case, she should have discovery. (Don't confuse this with going to court on the procedural issue of whether the district would be obligated to conduct the investigation without her cooperation.) That would be available only if an investigation were undertaken. Amy, therefore, agreed to be interviewed and cooperate with the investigation.

7

TACTICAL MANEUVERS TO OBTAIN THE GREATER GOOD

Amy allowed the investigation by the district's law firm. It might have seemed to the district that it had scored points by getting her to cooperate. Long before Amy agreed to cooperate with the district's investigation, however, she had engaged in a tactic that proved to be quite beneficial to her case. Amy simultaneously filed actions with the district's affirmative action officer and the attorney general's office, division on civil rights. The investigation undertaken by the division on civil rights involved its obtaining significant and discoverable materials from the district. This was information Amy truly wanted to review.

Even though Amy had been trained in the law, she was uncertain about certain areas in this matter. She felt it appropriate to obtain the services of an outside attorney. They consulted on the matter, and they agreed that the discovery able to be obtained by the division on civil rights would be crucial in prosecuting any case of discrimination Amy would choose to file in court. There was one hitch, however; the only way Amy could obtain the discovery the district had provided to the division on civil rights was if the case she filed with the division was concluded. This conclusion would either be a dismissal by the division or her withdrawal of the complaint.

The division had only recently commenced the investigation of the matter. It would be months, maybe even a year, before the division would determine the outcome of its investigation. Amy knew that the way to win a complaint against a school district on the grounds of discrimination could be found in, and probably existed in, the district's own documentation and practices. Amy was sure that if she could just get a look at the documentation provided by the district to the division, she could find what she was looking for. She, therefore, had to make a very serious decision.

After consultation with her attorney and much soul-searching, Amy decided to withdraw her complaint with the division on civil rights. She knew she was taking a risk, but she desperately needed to see this documentation. The only way she would be able to do so was if the case in the division was concluded. Amy, therefore, instructed her attorney to advise the division on civil rights that she was withdrawing her complaint. Amy then received a notice from the regional manager of the attorney general, division on civil rights, that her complaint had been withdrawn.

After Amy received the confirmation that her complaint had been withdrawn, she requested all the discovery the division had obtained from the school district. She waited for several weeks even before the division acknowledged her request. Amy didn't realize the volume of documents the district had provided the division in her case. She learned a lot about the requirement of an organization to conform to statutory requirements delineated in state statutes regarding affirmative action and anti-discrimination practices. The state promulgated several requirements on organizations of a certain size to make itself transparent regarding its hiring and promotion practices.

For example, federal affirmative action requires that any employer having fifty or more employees must have a written affirmative action plan on file and proof of submission. The affirmative action plan establishes compliance guidelines for recruiting, hiring, and promoting women and minorities to eliminate the present effects of past employment discrimination. The affirmative action plan must have an organizational analysis, which is based on an organization chart showing each manager or administrator, the job title of each employee who reports to that manager or administrator, and the race and gender of each employee.

The organization must also have on file a job group analysis, in which all departments are identified in the organization along with the jobs contained in each, the number of employees, the race and gender of each employee, and the job groups in the organization. The organization must also have an availability analysis on file. This is intended to determine the percentage of females and minorities who are theoretically available to the employer from the following three sources:

1. The percentage of females and minorities having the requisite skills and constituting part of the workforce in the employers' recruiting area for each job group. This data is available from the US Census Bureau and state unemployment benefit administrative agencies.
2. The percentage of female and minority employees the employer has already employed in feeder groups. "Feeder groups" is defined as other job groups from which promotions have been or recently could be made.
3. The percentage of female and minority students attending educational and training institutions located in the employer's recruiting area for each job.[7]

---

[7] 41 C.F.R. Section 60-2.12

The organization is also required to have a "Utilization Analysis" on hand. This compares the percentage of female and minority employees currently employed in each job group to the overall availability of female and minority employees and a determination of whether there is underutilization in each group. This is simply a determination of whether the percentage of female and minority employees is less than would be expected based on the availability analysis.

The organization is also required to set goals and identify problem areas. Specific hiring and promotion goals must be identified and documented for each job group in which females or minorities are underutilized. These groups are designed to be sure that qualified females and minorities are considered in all hiring and promotion decisions. Identification of problem areas requires a review of all employment policies and practices to determine whether there is discrimination or whether a practice might discriminate against or discourage available minority and/or women employees. This documentation isn't merely window dressing. The employer has a responsibility to utilize this information. The employer has a responsibility to implement actions that will allow the organization to realize the previously arrived-at goals. Top management must be committed to and manifest support for the affirmative action process and manager education and training to ensure managers who make hiring and promotion decisions are fully aware and supportive of the affirmative action plan.

The employer must also engage in an "Analysis of Employment Activity." This is an annual statistical analysis of hiring, firing, layoffs, promotions, and transfers to determine whether these processes are resulting in more or fewer women and minorities in each job group. This analysis includes an "Adverse Impact Analysis," a statistical analysis of the employers hiring, firing, and promotions during the past year to determine whether an adverse impact may have occurred. To assist in conducting an adverse impact analysis, the employer is required to keep an applicant flow log, which identifies each applicant by position applied for, gender, and race to the extent that the employer can gather this information by inviting applicants to self-identify.

Through the Civil Rights Act of 1964, the Vocational Rehabilitation Act of 197 (sections 503–504), and various other acts, the federal government requires that no individual be discriminated against on the basis of race, color, national origin, sex, age, or disability. The US Department of Education, the Office of Civil Rights, monitors discrimination complaints; and the US Department of Justice and the US Department of Labor monitor employment-related issues. The federal government may at any time audit an employer to determine whether he or she is in compliance with the rules and dictates of the civil rights statutes. It focuses on employers who have at least 150 employees. Most school districts fall into this category.

For further information regarding the foregoing and the requirements of affirmative action plans, consult the following:

- Affirmative Action History: http://www.infoplease.com/spot/affirmative1.html[8]
- Debate on Affirmative Action: https://youtube/zm5QVcTI2I8[9]
- History of Affirmative Action (Timeline)[10]

---

[8] Borgna Brunner, Beth Rowen, and Logan Chamberlain, "Affirmative Action History," Infoplease.com, January 25, 2020, https://www.infoplease.com/history/us/affirmative-action-history.

[9] Hasan Minhaj, "Affirmative Action," *Patriot Act with Hasan Minhaj*, Netflix, posted October 28, 2018, YouTube video, 21:47, https://youtu.be/zm5QVcTI2I8.

[10] History of Affirmative Action, video excerpt streamed from Affirmative Action Methodology Series 101, YouTube – Biddle Consulting Group – January 17, 2012, https://YouTube.com

You can see from the foregoing that significant attention is paid to an organization's promotion of affirmative action. The organization is required to prove its adherence to policy and law by the creation and maintenance of documentation that supports this requirement. The foregoing primarily concerned itself with the federal requirement for certain organizations to document their support of affirmative action. Many states have their own requirements for the support of affirmative action.

You should realize that not only is this requirement promulgated for general organizations of a certain size, but some requirements exist specifically for school districts. For example, in the state of New Jersey, there is a specific code requirement for adherence to and observation of affirmative action in public schools. That is in the New Jersey Administrative Code section entitled, "Managing for Equality and Equity in Education."[11] Although primarily concerned with equal access to educational programs and services by district boards of education for school students, it also requires equality and equity in employment and contract practices. This refers to all policies and practices governing the recruitment, hiring, assignment, evaluation, retention, and promotion of a school's employees.

The consistent theme of this work, aside from discrimination and affirmative action and the necessity of organizations to conform and adhere to the dictates of affirmative action, is your ability to assert, establish, and prove you were discriminated against. It's a certainty that no manager, supervisor, director, superintendent, or board member is going to say, "Hey, I am going to discriminate against you and prevent you from obtaining what you have applied for on the basis of your race, creed, color, etc." That would be direct evidence of discrimination. There

---

[11] N.J.A.C. 6A:7-1 et. seq.

was a time in our country when people of ill will directly stated that no person of a certain race, religion, color, and so forth was welcome or able to apply for a position. This racism still exists, probably worse than before, but it is much more subtle and has gone mostly underground.

Discrimination is currently most efficiently established by the use of circumstantial evidence—that is, evidence that doesn't directly establish a proposition. Given the nature of the circumstances and in combination with other circumstantial evidence, however, a neutral, detached, and fair-minded fact finder could reasonably conclude that such not only existed but also was most likely the reason for the failure of a candidate to be hired or promoted. The reason this is important is because it establishes the need for the review of documents and the investigation of your district. You must obtain discovery and review it with particularity. A powerful, inescapable piece of circumstantial evidence to establish the existence of discrimination is the lack of the district's adherence to the statutory and/or code requirements for accountability in maintaining required records and documented procedures. The New Jersey law provides, in pertinent part, the following:

6A:7–1.9 Accountability

(a) The district board of education's obligation to be accountable for the chapter's requirements is not precluded or alleviated by any rule or regulation of any organization, club, athletic association, or other league or group.

(b) Each school district shall complete a comprehensive equity plan that includes a cohesive set of policies, programs, and practices that ensure high expectations, positive achievement patterns, and equal access to education opportunity for all learners, including students and teachers.

(c) A comprehensive equity plan shall include the following:

1. An assessment of the school district's needs for achieving equity in educational programs. The assessment shall include staffing practices, quality-of-program 14 data, stakeholder-satisfaction data, and student assessment and behavioral data disaggregated by gender, race, ethnicity, limited English proficiency, special education, migrant, date of enrollment, student suspension, expulsion, child study team referrals, preschool-through-grade-12 promotion/retention data, preschool- through-grade-12 completion rates, and re-examination and re-evaluation of classification and placement of students in special education programs if there is overrepresentation within a certain group;

2. A description of how other Federal, State, and school district policies, programs, and practices are aligned to the comprehensive equity plan;

3. Progress targets for closing the achievement gap;

4. Professional development targets regarding the knowledge and skills needed to provide a thorough and efficient education as defined by the New Jersey Student Learning Standards (NJSLS), differentiated instruction, and formative assessments aligned to the NJSLS and high expectations for teaching and learning; and

5. Annual targets that address school district needs in equity in school and classroom practices and are aligned to professional development targets.

(d) The comprehensive equity plan shall be written every three years.

(e) The district board of education shall initiate the comprehensive equity plan within 60 days of its approval and shall implement the plan in accordance with the timelines approved by the Department.

(f) If the district board of education does not implement the comprehensive equity plan within 180 days of the plan's approval date, or fails to report its progress annually, sanctions deemed to be appropriate by the Commissioner or his or her designee shall be imposed. Sanctions may include action to suspend, terminate, or refuse to award continued Federal or State financial assistance, pursuant to N.J.S.A. 18A:55–2.[12]

Most states have a similar provision in its statutory or administrative code. The requirement of school districts to adhere to the foregoing is mandatory. If it is established that the school district has failed to adhere to, implement, or provide for any of the provisions, that is substantial circumstantial evidence that the school district engages in discrimination. In fact, outside of direct evidence, such evidence is probably the best evidence to establish this, and it is the kind of evidence the district won't be able to refute, overcome, or explain away.

After a review of the discovery the school district provided to the division of civil rights and an extensive analysis thereof, Amy discovered what she was looking for. Her hard work paid off. What she found was evidential in nature and satisfied the requirements of circumstantial evidence. Let's talk about the doctrine of circumstantial evidence.

---

[12] N.J.A.C. 6A:7–1.9

Those who are interested in an alleviation of racism in the workplace in general and the elimination of discrimination in hiring and promotion in particular have involved themselves with an analysis of the phenomenon and the ability of someone who has been the victim of discrimination to prove or successfully assert that he or she was the victim thereof. In other words, how would someone who was aggrieved by a purported act of discrimination establish such? A person, group, or entity who sets out to avoid hiring people of a certain race, religion, color, or creed won't directly say they are going to refrain from hiring or promoting a person because of that reason.

Those bent on an insidious practice of discrimination and are determined to keep members of certain groups out of their organization realize that a direct approach toward that end generally not only would not succeed but also would threaten their job status and profession. If their actions were outrageous enough, they might find themselves prosecuted and face jail time or substantial fines. Those who are interested in this practice must be very careful and subtle in these undertakings. That is the difference between direct evidence and circumstantial evidence of discrimination. This was briefly discussed before.

The easiest and simplest way to illustrate the doctrine of direct and circumstantial evidence is the following simple example. Let's say the defendant is accused of murder; an essential element is that the defendant killed the victim. At trial, the prosecutor elicits testimony from a witness, who says she saw the defendant shoot the victim and that the victim died.

That witness's testimony is direct evidence that the defendant killed the victim. Other elements must be adduced to establish murder, but a major burden has been overcome: the fact that the victim died, and that the defendant killed him or her. Let's say we have the same facts, but this time no one saw the defendant shoot the victim. The prosecutor puts a witness on the witness stand who says he heard the defendant say the defendant was going to kill the victim. The next witness the prosecutor puts on the witness stand testifies that he sold the defendant a gun that employed the same caliber bullets as the caliber of bullet that killed the victim. The next witness says that immediately after the death of the victim, he saw the defendant with blood on his hands and shirt. The next witness is a police officer, who arrived when the man who saw the defendant with blood on his hands and shirt called the police. This police officer found the defendant and conducted a paraffin test to determine whether there was gunpowder on his hands. The test came back positive.

In the last scenario, there is no direct evidence of the defendant shooting the victim. There is, however, a significant amount of circumstantial evidence the prosecutor has introduced in an attempt to have the jury look at all the evidence in tandem and make a determination whether all these factors and this evidence lead to a reasonable conclusion that the defendant shot the victim. Both types of evidence are admissible in a court of law. Direct evidence is easier, but sometimes circumstantial evidence is just as convincing as direct evidence, if not more so.

The individuals who drafted anti-discrimination legislation realize there will hardly ever be direct evidence of discrimination. Discrimination will undoubtedly need to be established by the use of circumstantial evidence. The circumstances surrounding the employer's actions toward the victim of discrimination will need to be analyzed to see whether a reasonable person could conclude that the person was denied what he or she sought because of discrimination. With this in mind, the Supreme Court created a test to allow a plaintiff in a discrimination case to establish a prima facie (Latin meaning "on its face" or "at first glance") case though based on circumstantial evidence.

This is important because of the rules of trial procedure. The plaintiff as the complaining entity must carry the burden of proof in the matter. That simply means the plaintiff must create a scenario that amounts to a real controversy allowing for a jury's determination.

The plaintiff initiates the action in a civil case. Even before the trial starts, the plaintiff must establish a pleading (complaint) that will amount to a cause of action, a prima facie case. The plaintiff files the complaint with the court and serves it on the defendant. The defendant answers, usually in a stream of denials. If the plaintiff fails to allege enough facts in the pleadings of allegations of wrongdoing or fails to establish a prima facie case, the other side, the defendant (in this case, the school district) will ask the court to end the matter right then. That is called "summary judgment."

A motion for summary judgment is usually filed by the defendant after the defendant files an answer, but if no real controversy is alleged in the complaint, the defendant might ask for a summary judgment (dismissal) before an answer is filed. If the summary judgment is granted, the case is over. If the summary judgment motion is denied before an answer is filed, an answer must follow; if after the answer, the discovery process commences. We previously discussed discovery; as a reminder, it is simply an exchange of proofs that each side will give the other and use to establish its own point of view.

The school district of which Amy was a member employed the device of the interview as its main device for the justification of hiring and promotion. The follow-up interviews and queries she tendered to the superintendent of schools when she was denied a promotion to principal routinely gave the same answer: "You just didn't perform in the interview as well as others did." One of the documents Amy obtained from the division on civil rights after she dismissed the complaint was a breakdown of the scores each interviewee received after one of the interviews for a principal vacancy.

This document was the tally sheet of the interviews conducted for a specific opening. It listed the names of all the candidates including Amy's. It also showed the time of the interview, whether the interview's purpose was to fill an elementary school position or a middle school position (both of which were open at the time), the score each member of the interview committee gave to the candidate (located in the comment section), and the tally of all the scores for that candidate. What Amy discovered after reviewing the breakdown of the scores of each of the candidates for principal, as reflected on that sheet, was most revealing.

Located on the far-right side of the tally sheet was the sum of the scores each of the five members of the interview committee gave to each candidate. Amy noticed that the highest score a candidate achieved was 213. If the interview process had meant anything, that person should have gotten the position, but he or she didn't get the job. In fact, the person who scored 158 got the job. Amy was now convinced that the fix was in and that the interview process had been a complete sham. It hadn't been designed to identify and/or appoint the most qualified person to the position and had been mere window dressing in an attempt to make the process look legitimate.

Amy knew it was almost impossible to prove employment discrimination by direct evidence. It is almost always a matter of circumstantial evidence. The US Supreme Court, mindful of the difficulty in establishing a prima facie case of discrimination by direct evidence promulgated a test to be used to establish whether a case of employment discrimination based solely on circumstantial evidence would be allowed to proceed past summary judgment. In other words, it set down a set of rules that must be adhered to for a case of this kind to be able to get to a jury and not be dismissed after the pleadings have concluded.[13]

In the case of *Anderson v. Exxon Corp.*,[14] the New Jersey Supreme Court, relying on the United States Supreme Court holdings, indicated that the plaintiff had the initial burden of production. To establish a prima facie case of discrimination, the plaintiff must show that

1. the plaintiff is in a protected class.
2. the plaintiff was qualified for the work for which he or she applied.
3. the plaintiff wasn't hired or promoted; and
4. the employer promoted someone with the same or lesser qualifications who wasn't in a protected status.

The analysis doesn't end there, however. Once the foregoing is accomplished, the burden of production shifts to the employer to show that the employer has a legitimate, nondiscriminatory, business justification for the decision to promote whomever the employer promoted. After that, the burden shifts back to the plaintiff to assert and establish that the reason the employer proffered for promoting whomever it did was a "mere pretext" and that the real reason was discrimination.

Let's analyze Amy's case in light of the *Anderson* case.

1. She fell within a protected class. She was Hispanic American.
2. She was qualified for the work she had applied for. See number four below.
3. She wasn't promoted.

---

[13] McDonald Douglas v. Green, 411 U.S. 792 (1973); Griggs v. Duke Power Co., 401 U.S. 424 (1971)

[14] 89 N.J. 483, 446 A.2d 486 (1982)

4. The district promoted someone with the same or lesser qualifications who wasn't in a protected status. The successful candidate was a Caucasian female teacher, who had never had any administrative experience and whose highest degree was a master's degree. Amy had four university degrees, including two doctorate degrees (a Bachelor of Arts or BA, a Master of Arts or MA, a juris doctorate or JD, and a doctorate in education or EdD). Amy had been an administrator (vice principal) for seven years at the time of the interviews.

Since the burden promulgated in *Anderson* had been met, the burden of production shifted to the school district to establish a legitimate, nondiscriminatory business justification for the decision to promote this person. Their legitimate, nondiscriminatory reason was that the successful candidate had performed better in the interview process. The burden of production then shifted back to Amy to establish that the asserted legitimate, nondiscriminatory reason for hiring the person was mere pretext and that the real reason was discrimination. This is where discovery and an investigation of the school district documents became so important.

Amy found the tally sheet of one of the interviews the district undertook to fill a principal vacancy. This wasn't the tally sheet used in the interview she participated in that led to the hiring of the person to whom she previously referred, but it doesn't matter. The successful candidate in that interview process received a score of 158. The highest score a candidate achieved was 213. However, the highest scoring candidate didn't get the promotion. Amy's argument was that the assertion that she hadn't been unsuccessful because she didn't perform as well in the interview process as the successful person was "mere pretext"; the tally sheet evidence made it apparent that the interview process meant nothing or very little. If the interview process had meant something, the person who scored 213 would have been the successful candidate, not the one who had the lower score of 158. Amy was free to argue, therefore, that the real reason for her failure to be promoted was race discrimination.

Remember, relentlessness and perseverance are the keys to success in an employment discrimination case or any case in which bias or favoritism or both is alleged. If Amy were to pursue this matter in the superior court, the foregoing proofs would satisfy the requirements of a prima facie showing and get her before a jury.

This is a significant hurdle in any civil case. Summary judgment has ended many civil cases. This fact is quite debilitating regarding the time and effort one must put in just to get to that level. Amy wasn't finished with her allegations against the district, however. The allegation previously discussed was one of constitutional law. Being relentless and filing all possible causes of action, Amy then decided to explore her options according to contract law.

The agreement between a board of education and a collective bargaining organization, such as an education association or an administrators' and supervisors' association, is nothing more than a contract. The definition of *contract* is an agreement between two parties where a meeting of the minds is established, and in which bargained for, legal detriment (consideration) exists.[15] "Bargained for, legal detriment" or "consideration" simply means that each party in a contract gives up something to obtain something. An employment contract usually has as its consideration that workers will perform duties and employers will pay and provide benefits. Neither one has to do the thing, but each gets something; the school district gets

---

[15] Ballantine, James A., and William S. Anderson, 1969, Ballantine's Law Dictionary, with pronunciations, Rochester, NY – Lawyer's Co-Operative Publishing Company.

the services which the employee gives up, and the employee gets pay and benefits which the school district gives up.

Amy advised the district through its attorney that the district, pursuant to one of its interview sessions, had violated certain provisions of the contract between the board of education and the administrators' and supervisors' association. The provisions provided that when an opening for employment in the school district occurred, the district would post each position separately and accept applications for each. It would undertake a separate application and hiring process for each.

Amy knew that, pursuant to one posting, the district had hired two principals, but it had held only one interview session. This was a clear violation of the agreement between those two parties. In the letter, Amy pointed out that, notwithstanding that the statute of limitations had prevented her from bringing this as a separate cause of action in any lawsuit she would bring, she would certainly make a motion before the court to allow its introduction as evidence of the district's continuing and repetitive pattern of violation of laws, rules, policy, and contract provisions. Amy knew of others in the district who knew of improprieties the district had engaged in in its hiring and promotion practices. This was a continuation of the theme she had advanced of being relentless and all-encompassing in the pursuit of her rights.

Amy's grievance against the school board culminated in her appearance before the school board to directly plead her case. Very soon after she appeared before the school board, she was notified that the relief she sought had been denied. Having voluntarily dismissed the Equal Employment Opportunities Commission (EEOC) and the division on civil rights complaints, and now being advised that her grievance against the board had been denied, one would think she was out of options and had to acquiesce and live with the obvious unfairness and impropriety of a racist and biased organization. If you thought that, you did not know Amy.

8

EPILOGUE TO PART 1

The formal actions Amy had promulgated against the school
district had come to an end. Her best shot at achieving satisfaction
against the school district was pursuant to the Equal Employment
Opportunities Commission complaint in conjunction with the division
on civil rights complaint. Additionally, her grievance against the school
district was grounded in its breach of the agreement between the
administrator's and supervisor's association and was also a substantial
cause of action. As indicated, Amy dismissed the complaints filed with
the EEOC and the division on civil rights. Concomitantly, the school
board denied her grievance against it.

Amy investigated other possibilities for action against the school
district. She researched the possibility of filing a tort action against the
school district. A tort in law is a special cause of action. It is defined as
"a wrong independent of contract; a breach of duty which the law, as
distinguished from a mere contract has imposed. An injury or wrong

committed either with or without force, to the person or property of another"[16]

A tort is distinguishable from a breach of contract, in that the latter arises under an agreement of the parties, whereas the tort is ordinarily a violation of a duty fixed by law, independent of contract or the will of the parties.

The nature of the cause of action Amy contemplated against the school district arising from tort was an allegation that the school district, by depriving her of a position she was not only clearly qualified for but also more qualified for than the actual successful candidate, had caused an intentional infliction of emotional distress against her. This is a cause of action recognized in tort. Amy's further research indicated that, in order to file a course of action in tort against a public entity such as the school district, she would have to make a claim pursuant to the Tort Claims Act. In common law (on which American law is based, derived from English law), one couldn't sue the sovereign. In England, the sovereign was the king, queen, or other head of government. The proposition that one couldn't sue the king, queen, or other monarch is based on the Latin maxim *Rex Non-Potest Pecarre* "the King Can do no Wrong."[17]

If the king can do no wrong, no cause of action can exist against him. In our society today, the sovereign is the government. Generally, one cannot sue the government unless it agrees to allow a suit against it. Both state and federal government, recognizing that significant injustice might occur if blanket immunity existed for the government, its minions, and its employees regarding tort actions, has allowed itself

---

[16] Ballantine, James A., and William S. Anderson, 1969, Ballantine's Law Dictionary, with pronunciations, Rochester, NY – Lawyer's Co-Operative Publishing Company

[17] Russell v. Inhabitants of Devon, 100 English Reporter, 359 (1788 - Kings Bench); Mower v. Leicester, 9 Mass. 247 (1812)

to be sued under certain circumstances. Both in the federal government and in certain state governments, such suits are referred to as tort claims and are governed under the Tort Claims Acts. In New Jersey, for example, the law is <u>N.J.S.A.</u> 59:1–1, CLAIMS AGAINST PUBLIC ENTITIES.

To maintain an action against the government, specifically a school district, a plaintiff must establish four elements.

1. Intentional and outrageous conduct by the defendant, the school district. Such conduct must either be intentional or reckless in deliberate disregard of a high degree of probability that emotional distress will follow.

2. The defendant school district's conduct must be extreme and outrageous. It must be so outrageous in character and extreme in degree as to go beyond all possible bounds of decency and be regarded as atrocious and utterly intolerable in a civilized community.

3. The defendant school district's actions must have been the proximate cause of a plaintiff's emotional distress.

4. The emotional distress suffered by the plaintiff must be so severe that no reasonable person could be expected to endure it.[18]

The standard for the maintenance of such a cause of action is so high and the proofs so specific that Amy would never have been able to establish the criteria for the sustenance of such a lawsuit. The standard essentially required the plaintiff to be completely incapacitated and incapable of a normal life because of the defendant's actions. Amy immediately discounted consideration of such a cause of action.

---

[18] Buckley v. Trenton Savings Fund Society, 111 N.J. 355, 366–367 (1988); Taylor v. Metzger, 152 N.J. 490, 516 (1997)

In conclusion of this part, please acknowledge the following courses of action Amy filed or considered:

1. Two grievances against the board of education
2. Two filings with the EEOC and the civil rights division of the attorney general's office
3. Considered filing under the New Jersey Tort Claims Act

Relentlessness and persistence are the key. Let the employer know you will never give up and will pursue any and all possible causes of action against it.

The superintendent of schools serving during the time Amy was pursuing her rights abruptly left the district with little advanced notice. A new superintendent was appointed. Approximately a month later, the new superintendent of schools, the assistant superintendent before this, arrived at Amy's office in the middle school. She was shocked not only that the new superintendent appeared in her office unannounced and unbeknownst to her but also by what he said to her.

His conversation primarily consisted of small talk. He was getting to something, but Amy couldn't figure out what it was. Every time it seemed like he was going to get to the point, he diverted his conversation to something else. He was clearly uncomfortable. Finally, he indicated to Amy that he and the school board realized that she was unhappy. He tried to elicit from her whether she would be filing any more actions against the board. Amy didn't directly answer but hinted that this was extremely likely. He became grave in his expression. He told Amy that this decision wouldn't benefit anyone, that all these filings would tie up the school board with business outside the education of young people. Amy indicated to him that if the school board had acted fairly, none of this would be necessary.

After a significant pause, he looked Amy straight in the eye and said, "What do you want, Amy?" She said that she thought what she wanted was obvious: a principalship. He said to her that no principalship was available at that time. He said the school board might possibly look favorably on an application from her when a principalship opened. He then asked what could be done for her in the meantime. He said he knew of the circumstances surrounding Amy's leaving the high school. He said that he knew that Amy's office and accommodations at the high school were significantly superior to the meager accommodations that she had to abide by in the middle school. He indicated that he knew, because of this, that she had considered her transfer to be the previous superintendent's retaliation because of her filing the complaint with the EEOC. He also indicated that he was able to transfer her back to the high school if she so wished.

Although adopting a stoic veneer, Amy was flabbergasted. She had thought when she first saw him that he was going to engage in retaliation for all the actions Amy had filed against the board. She thanked him and indicated that, though she wasn't happy in the middle school, she didn't want to return to the high school. Amy told him that since there were many more elementary schools in the district than there were secondary schools, and the odds favored an opening for principal in the elementary schools, she would like a transfer to an elementary school. She opined that she could learn the elementary protocols if an opening for a principal came about. She said that if such an opening appeared, she would be ready. He said to her that it would be done.

In the next school board minutes, there was an annotation transferring Amy from the middle school to an elementary school. Amy thereafter took up her position as vice principal of an elementary school, where she served until an elementary school principal went on maternity leave. There was an opening for a maternity leave principal replacement. Amy applied for the job, and she was successful. That summer there was an opening for a full-time principal. After six years of trying, several applications, numerous interviews and many filings against the school district, Amy finally became a full-time principal.

It cannot be disputed that Amy's persistence paid off. None of the filings she undertook with the EEOC, the civil rights complaint, the grievance procedures, her exploration of notice of actions under the contract liability statutes, or her intention to file pursuant to the Tort Claims Act had any direct ability to allow her to achieve what she wanted. It cannot be disputed, however, that these filings took a significant toll on the board. The time, resources, finances, especially in legal fees, and the general distraction of these filings to the school board in her opinion were the indirect cause of her ascendancy to a principalship.

It cannot be factually established that Amy's actions caused the departure of the superintendent of schools. It is extremely coincidental that the superintendent left in one month, and in the next month, the new superintendent met with her. Amy was very curious about the circumstances surrounding the previous superintendent's departure. Her belief was that the board had had enough of her constant filings and confrontations. The board might have instructed the previous superintendent to appoint her to the next principalship. That superintendent most likely declined. Amy thought that, along with what she believed was a very damning report regarding the affirmative action and equal opportunity penchant of the school district, might have caused a failure of her contract renewal.

Amy found out that although the superintendent was re-appointed, the superintendent resigned the month after her re-appointment was reflected in the school board meeting minutes. It is a rare thing for a superintendent of schools to leave a school district and go to another school district, especially if the superintendent is re-appointed. Usually, superintendents retire from the district. A superintendent with decades of experience in the system is sometimes more powerful in the city than the mayor. A superintendent might voluntarily leave a school district even if re-appointed if he or she believes that he or she has lost the confidence of the school board. This might be the case here.

Never forget that you are an educator. You invested significant time, money, effort, blood, sweat, and tears to get where you are. If you are worth it, go for it. Don't allow the "old-boy network" to stop your career progression or ambition. Make yourself invaluable. Go back to school. Get advanced degrees and additional certification. Make it impossible for the board to justify denying you your upward mobility. If you give in, you acquiesce.

PART 2

9

SUPERINTENDENCY AND THE "OLD BOY" NETWORK REVISITED

T he superintendent of schools who had elevated Amy to principal abruptly left the district. The swiftness of his departure and the secrecy surrounding his accepting a position in a different school district allowed for the proposition that his departure wasn't amicable. A vacancy in the superintendent's office was created. The local newspaper ran a notice of the opening for an interim superintendent. It asked any interested and qualified person to submit a cover letter of interest, résumé, and proof of certification for the position. Believing herself qualified, Amy applied for the position by sending the requested documentation. She addressed her letter and documentation to the president of the board of education.

The president of the school board had been a local businessman in the district for many years. He had retired from the school supply business a few years earlier. Amy's knowledge and information about the president of the board are relevant. Her previous exposure to the school district's unfortunate, discriminatory practices wasn't restricted to the filing of complaints and grievances. Amy had written an article published in a peer-reviewed magazine. This magazine, *School Practices of Importance*, is dedicated to the practice of school administration and is free to all members of the statewide principals' and supervisors' association. The title of the article is "The Old Boy Network Revisited: Friendship and Favoritism in the Public Schools."

The general thesis of the article is that discrimination has a deleterious effect on educational professionals. The article opined that this is especially true of educational professionals who dedicate themselves to their profession and expect to be able to contribute more to their school district as evidenced by their willingness to go the extra mile. The article suggested that this is reflected in the professional's desire for and accomplishment of the acquisition of additional and varied professional certificates, graduate and postgraduate degrees. It is also reflected, the article suggested, in the professional's willingness to work after school and on the weekends and engage in other activities that can only enhance his or her professional acumen to the benefit of his or her students.

The article provided insight into how slights visited on motivated and dedicated educational professionals of color can be devastating. It indicated how the professional might become exasperated, forlorn, depressed, and unmotivated. It delineated what the consequences might be if an educational professional concluded that his or her good works weren't worth anything to the school district. The essential conclusion of the article was that if the professional believed he or she was being taken for granted, he or she was likely to just "phone it in" and not provide a quality product. This might be intentional, but it could very well be subconscious. The additional thesis Amy advanced in the article was that because of the home rule nature of school districts in the state, many positions, especially those involving administration, went to the favored in the school district and almost always to members of a certain race.

The magazine in which Amy's article appeared was sent to every member of the state principals' and supervisors' association. This association is the statewide collective bargaining arm of the administrators of the public schools. The quarterly publication of this magazine and its dissemination to the state's public-school administrators are a benefit of membership. Each of these individuals, along with anyone interested in the public schools of the state, regularly read this magazine. That included the president of the board of education. Only two people responded to Amy's article. One was the president of the board of education.

It was a short message. It was sent from him to her by email, and it indicated his agreement with the general premise of Amy's article. He essentially said he recognized and agreed with Amy's proposition that unless and until public schools started to hire and promote based on merit rather than on familiarity, friendship, nepotism, and/or racism, the students would suffer. He continued by indicating that his sister and daughter, who was an educator, also agreed with the article and gave Amy high marks for it. Amy was very thankful, and in a return email, she indicated her appreciation for his feedback.

The president of the school board called a meeting of all the administrators and supervisors in the district in an attempt to explain the sudden departure of the superintendent and to indicate how they would proceed. This meeting was approximately a month after Amy applied for the interim superintendency. Amy had heard nothing from the district regarding her application for interim superintendent. There was no interview. There wasn't even an acknowledgment of receipt of her application and credentials. The assistant superintendent of schools led the meeting, though the president of the board of education attended it. The assistant superintendent of schools welcomed all of the administrators, supervisors and directors, and the first words out of her mouth after the welcome were that she had been appointed interim superintendent and that one of the directors in the district had been appointed interim assistant superintendent.

These individuals had been favored in the district for decades. The assistant superintendent, now the interim superintendent of schools, was a long-time employee of the district. When Amy and this person first met approximately several years earlier, this person had been a teacher, then an assistant principal, a principal of an elementary school, a principal of a middle school, and a principal of the high school. This person then became a supervisor in the district. Thereafter this person became assistant superintendent of schools. The new interim assistant superintendent of schools had previously been a teacher. Where he truly showed himself and became known in the district was with his prowess as a manager. He was very adept at management, a favored member of the district and especially by the new interim superintendent of schools.

Immediately after the meeting, Amy wrote to the president of the board of education. She indicated all her concerns regarding the way the interim superintendency and interim assistant superintendent positions had been filled. Among other things, she indicated her disappointment with him and her belief that what he had indicated to her in his reaction to her article was either a lie or evidence that he had been corrupted.

A couple of days later, the president of the board of education visited Amy in her office. He indicated that he thought there might have been a misunderstanding and that he was there to clear it up. He assured Amy that the position occupied by the interim superintendent was only on an emergency basis. He indicated that there would be no interim superintendent per se. He explained his belief that the person they were looking for to serve as interim superintendent was to be a retired superintendent who would be appointed temporarily.

He also said the board had someone in mind to occupy the interim superintendency who was indeed a retired superintendent but that person was unavailable. This person was a retired superintendent from another district. He also said that when the position was filled, it would be with an acting superintendent appointed for a specific term, and it would be filled only after a review of all the applications and interviews were held. Amy then asked about the interim assistant superintendent's position. He said that when the board appointed the person who was designated as interim superintendent, they gave that person the right to choose his or her own assistant.

Amy waited patiently for a phone call from the district regarding her interview or that they had considered her application and weren't going to offer her the position. The August school board minutes revealed that the person holding the position had been appointed acting superintendent and that the person holding the interim assistant superintendent position had been appointed acting assistant superintendent. Amy wrote a letter of objection and filed a grievance with the school board.

It looked as though the district was up to its old tricks. It wasn't that Amy was unsuccessful, hadn't even been considered for the position, or hadn't even been contacted about the position. The issue of considerable concern was that the president of the board of education had sat in her office and told her that the very thing that had happened wasn't going to happen. Amy had worked with this man when he was a school district supplier. They were close and had a very good, professional relationship. He and Amy had attended school supply conferences and workshops together. They had joked and shared personal stories about their lives and professions. This was a man who, when he retired and decided to run for the school board, had asked for Amy's help. By then Amy had been the principal of a school.

Every year Amy's school held its annual back-to-school night. During this event, Amy's "old friend", the present board president, appeared. At the time, he had just retired, and he advised Amy that he was going to run for the school board. During their conversation, he asked her to introduce him to the assemblage. While Amy was on the stage, addressing the parents and guardians, she took time out to introduce him as a man who had been a long-term friend and business associate of the school district, and he had just retired. She spoke very highly about this man. Amy indicated that she had worked with him for years, that his dedication to the district was beyond reproach, and that he was a local resident dedicated to education.

This book is designed to advise you educators and other employees of, among other things, your legal rights. It's important for you to realize that much of what I am indicating in this work transcends legality. It involves human relationships. Ultimately, it will be human beings who will decide whether you are hired or promoted. The most efficient way to ensure your upward mobility is to amass impeccable credentials and develop relationships. Be careful, however, because many people aren't who they seem. Many people develop relationships only to feather their own nests and step over people on their way to their goal. People can be deceptive; your credentials speak for themselves.

10

GRIEVANCE NUMBER THREE

Filing a grievance against one's employer is tricky business. When Amy filed her first grievances, the affirmative action officer, who was the entity with whom the grievance should be filed, had to disqualify himself. As was indicated, his disqualification was based on a conflict of interest. The conflict of interest was generated because he had sat on several of the committees that Amy had appeared before in an attempt to secure a principalship. The issue is whether the district designed it like that.

It always bothered Amy that the district's affirmative action officer had been allowed to sit on committees that would determine the filling of positions in the district. Her question was, "Didn't someone realize that having the affirmative action officer sit on interview committees to fill vacant positions in the district might cause a problem?" It seemed to Amy that this would have been at least a passing thought with those who were responsible for the appointment of an affirmative action officer and those responsible for setting up interview committees.

Amy's legal training caused her to think of a worst-case scenario with every issue. It occurred to her that this might have been the district's intention all along. Namely, by having the affirmative action officer (AAO) on interview committees and then having the result of the committee be contested, the AAO could always bow out from any investigation on the grounds of a conflict of interest and then appoint their favored candidate; someone who might find in their favor, no matter what the facts revealed. Someone like their paid legal counsel.

History may indeed repeat itself. Amy filed her grievance with the district affirmative action officer. It just so happened that the district affirmative action officer was also the president of the administrators' and supervisors' association of the school district. You guessed it! Conflict of interest. Obviously, the affirmative action officer of the school district, appointed by and working for the school district, cannot at the same time and in the same issue represent a member of the association of which he is the president, against the school district. The appropriate action for him was recusal from this matter based on the conflict. The affirmative action officer notified the school board that he was conflicted and, therefore, had to recuse himself. He then notified Amy in writing of this fact.

The New Jersey Administrative Code (NJAC), Title 6A, for example, promulgates the requirement that each school district in the state should develop an equity plan. It also requires each school district, pursuant to that plan, to appoint an affirmative action officer. If a district employee files a grievance against the district, in which it is alleged that the district has engaged in discriminatory behavior, that grievance is presented to the affirmative action officer. Although the administrative code doesn't set a time frame, it does indicate that, upon presentation of a complaint alleging discrimination, the affirmative action officer must immediately undertake an investigation. Amy notified the district of her contention that it had engaged in discriminatory conduct. The affirmative action officer immediately notified her about the conflict.

Let us review the discrimination complaint she had filed against the district years before; after the affirmative action officer notified her of the conflict, the district's attorney contacted Amy almost immediately to advise her that it would be taking up the investigation. Almost a month elapsed, and Amy heard nothing. She made several inquiries regarding the investigation, but no one in the central office could tell her anything. Amy reminded them of the necessity for an immediate investigation pursuant to the administrative code. She spoke to the superintendent, the business administrator, the assistant superintendent, and anyone else she thought might be able to shed some light on when this investigation would get underway and when she would be contacted. Then her instincts kicked in. Knowing the president of the board of education as well as she knew him, Amy got the distinct impression that he was engaging in gamesmanship.

It occurred to Amy that the president of the board of education wasn't going to request an investigation. She got the distinct impression that the board was waiting for her to file an action with the Equal Employment Opportunity Commission (EEOC) and/or the division on civil rights as she had previously done. Amy surmised that the board, rather than institute an investigation, would let her file her actions, allow whatever agency it was filed with to undertake the investigation, and merely respond. Knowing the president of the board like she did, Amy didn't think he was above such an underhanded scheme. In any event, she knew it was no accident that it was taking so long for an investigation to get underway.

If you intend to confront your employer, you must know who all the players are. Many school districts are governed by "home rule," which was discussed earlier. In a nutshell, that simply means most of the decisions made in the district are done so by the district with little to no interference from the state commissioner's office. The districts are not totally autonomous, however. The commissioner of education has a presence in every district in the form of an executive superintendent of schools. This person is in each county. Although all decisions made in the school district, except those specifically dictated by statute and/or code, are made by the school district, some must be approved by the commissioner's office in the person of the executive superintendent of schools.

One of the executive superintendent's obligations is to see to it that the statutes and codes that govern the schools are adhered to. This includes the requirements of equity in education. A month had transpired since Amy filed her grievance with the school board; since no investigation was being conducted, she contacted the executive superintendent. Amy wrote him a letter, telling him the school district was violating the administrative code requiring that an investigation be undertaken upon any allegation of discrimination practiced by a school district.

Approximately a week after she sent the letter, the county superintendent gave her a call. They spoke for a while. He wanted to know why Amy thought that the district wouldn't eventually investigate her claim. Amy responded that she knew who the players were in the district. She indicated that she had worked with the president of the board of education for years. Amy told him that her knowledge of him led her to believe he wouldn't undertake the investigation and would try to gain an upper hand. She told the county superintendent that almost ten years earlier, she had filed two separate actions against the district with the Equal Employment Opportunities Commission (EEOC), the division on civil rights, and the district's own affirmative action officer.

Amy told the executive superintendent that since she had previously filed actions in outside agencies, he possibly thought she would do so this time. He probably thought he would allow any agency she had filed a complaint with to take the investigation and that the board would merely respond. Because of her dealings with this man and his deception regarding his belief in the accuracy of the propositions in her article, Amy thought he might take the low road. The executive superintendent was very kind and indicated that he would look into the matter and get back to her.

A couple of days later, Amy got a phone call from a big, fancy law firm out of Washington, DC. They said the school district had retained them to investigate the allegations of race discrimination she had filed against the district. Amy couldn't help but smile. No district wants the commissioner's office interfering and meddling in their affairs. Amy imagined the conversation the executive superintendent of schools had with the president of the board of education. It might have gone something like this:

> It's come to our attention that a complaint was filed against your district alleging discrimination. I'm sure you are aware of the requirement of school districts to have its affirmative action officers investigate immediately upon receipt of a complaint of this nature. The complainant has contacted this office and has alleged that no investigation has been undertaken by you. The complaint alleges that almost a month has transpired since his initial complaint, and she has heard nothing regarding an investigation. We are sure this was merely an oversight on your part. We trust you

will expeditiously investigate this matter to prevent our office from getting directly involved. Thank you so much.

As previously indicated, the last thing in the world any "home rule" school district wants is the commissioner's office sniffing around. The commissioner's office, through the device of the executive superintendent, has wide discretion and even greater powers. If the commissioner gets inside a school district for any reason, it is going to investigate everything, not just the allegations of a single complaint. It is going to look at curriculum, budget, personnel, contracts, and every and any other thing it can think of. It will probably not leave until it finds something wrong, if for no other reason than to justify the expense of the investigation.

The board attorney contacted Amy soon thereafter and indicated that it wanted to interview her regarding her complaint. A few days later, two attorneys appeared in Amy's office. They interviewed her for two and a half hours.

Reference was previously made to the necessity of engaging your adversary in a procedurally correct manner. The procedures you will use are usually delineated in the agreement between your board of education and your collective bargaining unit. In matters of litigation and those involving the redress of grievances, the procedure with which you engage your adversary is almost as important as the substance of the allegations. In other words, if your procedural actions aren't in conformity with what the law requires or what the parties had previously agreed to, the substance of your allegations, even though they might be correct and completely on point, might never be addressed. Because Amy hadn't heard from the district involving its initiation of an investigation of her allegations, she revisited the agreement between the board of education and the collective bargaining unit.

Most agreements between boards of education and collective bargaining units spell out the grievance procedure. They usually refer to steps in the process. The steps one engages to obtain a redress of grievances are very important. This is because it is in everyone's best interest to attempt to resolve any grievance at the lowest level possible. Grievance procedures usually involve the grievant going to his or her immediate supervisor. If the grievance cannot be resolved there, it is taken to the next level and so on.

As a principal, Amy's next level would be the assistant superintendent, then the superintendent, and then the school board itself. This was a unique situation because the assistant superintendent she would immediately address was a party to the action. In other words, not only was the interim assistant superintendent not able to provide the redress she was seeking, but it was against him and the interim superintendent of schools that she sought redress. Therefore, to be correct in all respects, Amy notified the board of education itself of the conflict of interest of the interim assistant superintendent, and of the interim superintendent, and brought her grievance directly to it.

Amy drafted and served notice on the board of education with the knowledge and permission of the president of her collective bargaining unit. This is an important point. You should always keep your collective bargaining unit apprised of your actions. It would also be advisable to obtain permission from it regarding your actions. You will never know when you will need its power, influence, and good will.

It was also reviewed, acknowledged, and agreed to by the attorney the collective bargaining unit had consulted. Teachers and other school employees have a collective bargaining unit. The principals, supervisors, and directors have a separate collective bargaining unit. These local collective bargaining units are in touch with and regularly consult with state operatives who oversee and help the local collective bargaining units with such things as negotiations, agreements, pay scales, and other things.

After consultation with the state association and with notice to the executive board of her local collective bargaining unit, the associations attorney filed a "Request for Submission of a Panel of Arbitrators." The attorney emailed the board's attorney and indicated that an arbitrator had been assigned to Amy's grievance. She indicated a date for a hearing and requested that the attorney indicate whether she was available. Amy was delighted to receive these documents because they let the school board know she was deadly serious and intended to proceed in this matter.

Thereafter, Amy's attorney contacted the board's attorney after meeting with her. The board attempted to resolve the matter short of a hearing. Much to her surprise, Amy's attorney advised her that the board would be willing to settle the matter for a small, nominal payout to her. Amy was shocked by this offer. Her point was simple: she wasn't doing this for the money. Also, the board attorney had contacted her in early October regarding the commencement of the investigation by his law firm. Although considerable time had passed, neither Amy nor the attorney had heard anything about the results of the investigation. Her attorney pointed this out to their adversary and indicated that Amy wouldn't proceed without it.

A few weeks later, the district posted the position opening of the superintendent of schools in the local newspaper and on its website. This was to be a permanent position. Amy applied for the position. She was in an awkward position, however. After all, how does one apply to a school board for a position and sue the board at the same time? Even if the grievance were totally unrelated to the filling of the position, it would be awkward. Her grievance against the board related to the filling of the position of interim superintendent of schools. Amy wrote a letter to the board, indicating her interest in the permanent position of superintendent. She couched her language with great care. She indicated that she thought the qualifications the school board had delineated as being required for a successful candidate had been deliberately created to exclude her as a candidate. Amy indicated that she thought discrimination was still in play and that the district was up to its old tricks again.

One might ask, "Why would Amy bother to apply for the position? They denied her the interim position. Why would they consider giving her this position?" Amy did it for the record. As previously indicated, procedure is very important in litigation and in the filing and maintenance of grievances. If Amy didn't apply for the position, the first words spoken by the school board would be, "She did not get the position because she did not apply for it."

Much discussion was made regarding agreements between collective bargaining units. The issue of procedures of grievance in collective bargaining units should be revisited and reviewed. The collective bargaining agreement between the board of education and Amy's collective bargaining unit had a provision involving the procedure to undertake when filing a grievance. It indicated that any dispute would be resolved in house by the lowest level supervisor. The matter would go all the way to the board of education if it couldn't be resolved at a lower level. If the board of education refused to grant the relief sought, the matter would be submitted to arbitration. The problem with Amy's collective bargaining agreement was that the arbitration called for in the agreement was nonbinding. In other words, no matter what the arbitrator decided or recommended, neither side would be bound by it. Either side could therefore accept or reject it. To pursue this matter to arbitration, therefore, was an exercise in futility. Amy decided to forego the grievance and arbitration procedure and take a more direct route.

The attorney and Amy had several differences of opinion regarding matters of law. One of the major differences was regarding a doctrine called "collateral estoppel." In law, this is sometimes referred to as "estoppel by judgment" or "res judicata" Simply put, this doctrine indicates that if a matter has been disposed of in any forum of competent jurisdiction, that matter cannot be relitigated in another forum. It is the bar of a judgment against the relitigation of particular facts and issues but used sometimes to indicate a bar against the relitigation of a particular cause of action.[19] She indicated that even though the arbitration would be nonbinding and useless to obtain what Amy wanted, it would still be the adjudication of the matter in a forum of competent jurisdiction and therefore, incapable of Amy wished.

Simply put, she indicated that if the arbitrator ruled in Amy's favor, the school board could ignore the ruling and do nothing. It could certainly disallow the relief sought. She and Amy both agreed on this point and knew the board would never provide the relief sought. She also knew Amy intended to pursue the matter in the superior court. She opined that if the arbitrator ruled against Amy or ruled in her favor and the school board ignored the ruling, this would be a decision on the merits of the case, and further action by Amy in the superior court might be greeted by a motion to dismiss on the part of the district on the grounds of collateral estoppel—specifically that the matter had already been decided no matter the subsequent actions of either party.

Amy reviewed and researched the doctrine of collateral estoppel but found that she disagreed with the attorney on this point. She expressed her reasoning in a letter to the attorney. Amy was cautious, however. Even though she didn't agree that collateral estoppel applied in this

---

[19] Ballantine, James A., and William S. Anderson, 1969, Ballantine's Law Dictionary, with pronunciations, Rochester, NY – Lawyer's Co-Operative Publishing Company.

matter, she thought there was enough of an argument there for a judge to rule against her. She, therefore, withdrew her grievance and ended the matter there.

You must always remember that whenever you are pursuing an action that advances your rights, you must consider what comes next. You must be cognizant of your options should the present action fail. In that regard, the filing of a grievance and a course of action in court are like playing billiards. When you line up a shot in billiards, you aren't just considering making that shot. You are trying to get the ball in the pocket, but you want to position the other balls for the next shot. Some people call that "using English to position the balls where you want them."

You should also be aware that litigation is like chess. You sometimes know you are going to lose a piece to gain an advantage down the road. The key is to make sure what you gain down the road is not only accessible to you but also worth more than the piece you lost. Amy dismissed the case and immediately contacted the Equal Employment Opportunity Commission (EEOC). She filled out the paperwork required for the initiation of a complaint and received an inquiry number and an interview date and time.

The EEOC interviewed Amy, and she was prepared to proceed against the district. Before she could proceed, however, the district hired an Asian woman as its next superintendent of schools. This was the subtle, underhanded machination next used by the district to gain an advantage over her and her cause of action.

11

DECEPTION, DOUBLE-DEALING, DIABOLICAL DEEDS, AND OTHER PRACTICES OF ENTRENCHED EMPLOYERS

The underhanded and devious machinations of the school district are constantly at work. The basis of Amy's claim was that the district engaged in race discrimination by refusing to hire or even consider her candidacy for interim superintendent or superintendent, even though she was immensely qualified for the position. The district's hiring of an Asian American as superintendent of schools and the interim superintendent's resumption of his duties as assistant superintendent ended Amy's claim, since the cause of action was no longer legally or factually sustainable at law. This was because the new superintendent was a member of a protected class, referred to earlier in this book. When you take on an employer, it is good to remember that the employer always has a long memory and rarely forgives.

Soon after the appointment of the new superintendent, new personnel issues arose. The district hired a new human resources director, and one of their middle school principals left to take another job. The middle school principalship was available. Amy applied for it. Suddenly, a list of accusations, insinuations, and questions started wafting in the breeze. Complaints from faculty members assigned to her school started making their way to the human resources director and finally the superintendent. The complaints varied from unfair treatment to racism. This was very strange considering that Amy, a Hispanic American, was the principal of the school and that the complaints, according to them, had been generated by other minority faculty members.

Every year at its conclusion, each district employee whose employment is predicated upon possession of a state-issued certificate must submit to a final evaluation. This is a formal requirement in most school districts. This includes teachers, principals, assistant/ vice principals, supervisors, directors; all are subject to a summative observation and evaluation by the superintendent. Amy's summative evaluation meeting was the site of her newest and latest confrontation with the district.

The purpose of this annual meeting of all certificated faculty and staff in a school district is clear and prescribed by code and statute— namely to evaluate and discuss the evaluative, numeric score of the professional based on the year's professional practice and as reflected in an evaluative device containing rubrics on which the professional's performance is based. In that summative meeting, nothing else is germane; nor should it be discussed or broached.

As soon as she entered the superintendent's office for the summative evaluation and conference, the superintendent, along with the new HR director, left the issue of Amy's evaluation and proceeded to confront her regarding her application for the middle school position. The allegations ranged from allegedly unethical conduct on her part during the application process for principal to the purported negative climate at Amy's school. Apparently, Amy was being retaliated against for her previous filings against the district. The final cut was the superintendent's stated intention to reduce some of the scores in Amy's summative evaluation.

The superintendent's intention to reduce previously assessed, favorable scores and the allegation of unethical conduct in the application process (although such was never engaged in) put Amy in a difficult position. After all, the human resources director and the superintendent would be deciding whom to submit to the school board to fill the middle school position. Ultimately, they rejected Amy's application and hired the vice principal of the middle school. This person had no principal experience and was a little more than half Amy's age.

As previously asserted, when you go against an employer, you must be prepared for any devious, underhanded, and dirty trick imaginable. To meet these actions, you must employ an attack as the best defense. Amy responded to the lowering of good summative scores and allegations of unethical conduct by referring to code and statutory and case law. She acquainted herself with her rights pursuant to a summative meeting. She was entitled to rebut any adverse contentions. She did so and added a few claims, complaints, and allegations.

It was abundantly apparent that the district had no intention of appointing Amy to the middle school position. She was, however, surprised at the lengths with which it was willing to proceed to deny her the position. Giving her the one-two punch of accusing her of unethical conduct in her application for the position as well as lowering her summative score was a valiant, concerted effort to ensure that the district was under no obligation to offer her the position. Apparently, the district hoped Amy would just slink away with her tail between her legs. But that thought never occurred to Amy, and she prepared for another fight.

My advice is that in any attack against you, be it in your professional life, personal life, or anything else, you must respond swiftly and appropriately. Even in an allegation of improper professional conduct, especially if you are innocent, never go on the defensive. You must immediately mount a counterattack. Amy took this stance. She continued the barrage. She submitted an initial rebuttal to the president of the school board; another was coming, and it did. While the district was still absorbing, reeling from, and trying to figure out how to respond to Amy's initial rebuttal and notice of claims, she submitted a second rebuttal.

The premise of the second rebuttal was that, although according to the administrative code, the score in a summative evaluation couldn't be contested, the procedure by which the score had been arrived at could be contested and disputed. This fact is germane to a point made earlier: do your research and find out what is codified by law and statutorily required. Amy reviewed the superintendent and human resource manager's actions, compared them to what was allowed and required by law, and found that they had engaged in wholly improper and illegal actions.

As a result of their actions, Amy once again contacted the Equal Employment Opportunities Commission (EEOC) to file a formal complaint. Amy made online contact with the agency and was given an appointment for a telephonic intake interview. Amy decided to forego the district's internal grievance procedure. The procedure envisioned by the district was a no-win proposition for a grievant since it could result only in nonbinding arbitration. In other words, and as was previously explained, if the arbitrator decided in the grievant's favor, the ruling wasn't binding on the district, and it could simply ignore it.

It is another story, however, with the EEOC. There were many considerations in going this route. If a grievance was filed with the district, it would investigate pursuant to code but probably not too enthusiastically. Amy knew better than to trust an organization that investigated itself. The EEOC will conduct a very detailed and extensive investigation, including interviews, a demand for documents, a review of school policy and practice, a look at hiring and promotion practices, and much more. Also, as indicated in an earlier chapter, if the agency demands a document that isn't produced, the district would already have cast itself in a suspicious light.

Between the meeting that gave rise to her contacting the EEOC and her intake appointment with it, the district wasn't through with Amy yet. Difficult as it may be to believe, it undertook what she considered to be the worse, most foul, and most underhanded dealings one could imagine. When the previous superintendent resigned, the district sought an interim superintendent, a position for which Amy applied. But the district didn't even acknowledge Amy's application let alone granted her the favor of an interview. That was the substance of her grievance against the district, and that gave rise to her complaint of retaliation.

The district decided to make the assistant superintendent the interim superintendent after the president of the board of education told her that the district wouldn't be hiring any interim superintendent. It happens that that interim superintendent, along with the person she appointed as the interim assistant superintendent, solicited a district employee to follow Amy and keep a log of her actions. The document the employee compiled against Amy was negligently left where it could be found, and one of Amy's colleagues found the document and gave it to her. Amy held on to it but later found good reason to produce it. The employee was transferred to another school.

Amy's school sponsored a program she had created. This was a tutorial program. It was an after-school tutorial program that allowed students to get extra help with schoolwork. Many students stayed in school after the usual dismissal time. This is an accommodation for struggling students. The employee who had been solicited to compile information on Amy had, for years, worked for the tutorial program. In a conversation with former school employees, during which they were discussing the employee's transfer, they lamented not being able to associate with this employee. Amy overheard the employee reassure them that they would work together since she would be working in the tutorial program.

Amy contacted the director of the program and indicated her objection to this employee working in the tutorial program. She cited the fact that the district saw fit to transfer the employee to another school. She observed that the action must have been taken for some reason, which would be defeated should this employee be allowed to reenter the building, no matter the reason or cause. The director agreed. A few days later, the director called Amy and indicated the employee's very verbal objection to being denied working in the tutorial program. The director indicated that the employee contacted the human resources director and the superintendent. A meeting with the superintendent, the human resources director, the program director, Amy, and the employee was set.

On the day of the meeting, the superintendent gave the employee the opportunity to make her case for being part of the program at Amy's school. The employee expressed the proposition of her loyal service, honest work, and complete trustworthiness. When given the opportunity, Amy told the assemblage she didn't want this employee back in her building because she didn't believe she could trust the employee. Amy produced the log she had been given before the meeting that was the result of this employee's actions. This log listed some of Amy's movements and painted her in the most negative light one could imagine. Amy gave a copy to each person in the room.

Upon seeing the log, the employee became vocal. She didn't deny composing the document, but the employee's defense centered on how

Amy had obtained the document. The employee complained that Amy had rummaged through the employee's belongings to obtain the document and that this was a violation of the employee's privacy rights. Amy denied doing any such thing, and when the employee asked where Amy had gotten the document, Amy refused to tell her. The superintendent turned to the human resources director and said they had seen this document before.

Then a very strange thing happened. The employee, now in a fit of emotion, blurted out that the only one who should have had this item in his or her possession was the assistant superintendent of schools, who at the time of receipt of the document had been interim superintendent of schools. The employee blurted out that the interim superintendent of schools had asked her to engage in the following of Amy. The employee insisted that the interim superintendent, along with the interim assistant superintendent of schools, had engaged her to undertake this action.

Amy realized she had been presented with a statement by an employee of her school, whom the interim superintendent and interim assistant superintendent had commissioned. The purpose had been to defame, denigrate, and libel Amy for purposes only they knew but which Amy suspected. They obviously wanted to deny Amy any upward mobility in this district or any other. Amy's head was now swimming since the revelations emanating from this meeting were more than she could have imagined or hoped to learn.

The superintendent's statement that they had seen the document before led Amy to believe they had possessed this item during the pendency of her application for principal of the middle school, the denial of which had been the genesis of her notice of claim of retaliation and age discrimination. It occurred to her that a lot of effort had been undertaken, designed to keep her from any higher position and ultimately designed to cast an aspersion on her character and good name in the district.

After consideration of these revelations, Amy decided to notify the district, pursuant to the Tort Claims Act, that she intended to sue it, the interim superintendent, the interim assistant superintendent, and the employee for defamation of character. She filed a notice of claim with the president of the board of education.

It is appropriate at this point to briefly revisit the issue of the Tort Claims Act for the sake of understanding Amy's action as well as to provide an additional arrow for your quiver in your confrontation of those who would abuse, deny, or ignore you and your rightful quest toward professional achievement.

As stated earlier, the Tort Claims Act is a law that exists in every state and with the federal government. It lays down the proposition of "sovereign immunity." Succinctly put, it says the government or any part or entity of it cannot be sued. There is an exception to the general rule, however. The exception is that the government can be sued if it waives sovereign immunity and agrees to be sued. To sue the government under the act, one must notify it of the intention six months in advance of the filing of suit. This is called a "notice of claim."

The government by common law and statute lays down the general proposition that it cannot be sued. It then qualifies this statement by delineating circumstances by which it would subject itself to suit. One of these exceptions is that it will sometimes allow itself to be liable in a tort action. A tort, as you recall, is a wrongful act or an infringement of a right (other than under contract) leading to civil legal liability. An example of a tort is defamation of character. Defamation of character occurs when there is a publication of anything which is injurious to the good name or reputation of another person, or which tends to bring him into disrepute. Defamation can be broken down into two types: spoken, which is called "slander"; and written, which is called "libel."[20]

The document previously referred to was a compendium of lies, half-truths, and vicious insinuations solicited by Amy's superiors and compiled by an employee of the district. Since it was written, it could be properly characterized as libel.

I cannot overemphasize the depths to which your employer will go to keep you from actualizing your true potential if he or she doesn't want you to achieve it. The only issue is how you will react to the attempt by your employer. In any reaction, you must consider the probability of success and the risk you take in attempting to thwart employer actions.

Amy's initial memorandum to the school board had a three-fold purpose:

1. To notify the board that she had been legally and ethically wronged
2. To notify the board that she intended to seek redress for these wrongs
3. To give the board the opportunity to make her whole

The school board ignored Amy's notice. It didn't even discuss her contentions with her or acknowledge them. What any board or other employer does most often in a situation such as this is ignore it and hope the complainant will go away. To forget about the transgressions that had been perpetrated against Amy was the last thing on her mind.

After no contact from the school board, Amy determined that no response would be forthcoming. She then had to determine what

---

[20] Ballantine, James A., and William S. Anderson, 1969, Ballantine's Law Dictionary, with pronunciations, Rochester, NY – Lawyer's Co-Operative Publishing Company; Hollenbeck v. Hall, 103 Iowa 214, 72 NW 518.

her next course of action would be. Her previous dealings with the school board from years past revealed that it would be difficult, if not impossible, to secure legal representation to prosecute her claims. She was prepared to file a cause of action herself and proceed as a pro se litigant.

Amy searched the internet to find legal representation. She followed up with every lead. She cold-called, wrote letters, and made unscheduled visits to law offices. Amy did everything she could. As previously indicated, she had legal training and was, therefore, familiar with the rudiments of civil procedure.

Although sometimes necessary as a last resort, it is never a good idea for someone to represent himself or herself, even if that person is a lawyer or has legal training. If for no other reason, the logistics just don't work. How will you engage in direct examination of yourself at trial? Someone must question you to elicit testimonial evidence. The other issue involves the time involved in bringing a case, not to mention the legal nuances involved. Amy had neither the time nor the expertise in this branch of the law.

After months of searching, Amy was finally successful in obtaining legal representation. Amy and the attorney spoke several times for hours, during which she delineated all the wrongs she had endured over the years at the hand of the school board. Amy was very verbal in her delineation of the circumstances she had endured for years at the hands of the school district. After she provided written and verbal recounts, her attorney was completely apprised of her case.

Another point that must be made against representing yourself is what Amy's attorney did with the contentions she had raised. He promulgated theories of culpability that Amy had never thought or heard of. Amy was delighted and somewhat embarrassed that she hadn't raised these issues in the documentation provided to the board. She couldn't be too hard on herself, however, since she was a full-time educator. Although she possessed legal training, this wasn't her full-time, primary vocation. As stated, and for emphasis, only if left with no alternative should you proceed pro se. You must speak up and advance your rights, even if you must do so alone.

Amy's attorney drafted a summons and complaint and served it upon her adversaries. The matter proceeded through the state courts. This was further than she had ever gotten in her contentions against her employer. It wasn't a pleasant thing to be at odds with an entity one had a twenty-five-year relationship with. The sole purpose of this book is to apprise people who have invested years, tens of thousands of dollars, significant effort, and energy into creating a professional career, only to have an entity completely discount those resources, time, and efforts in favor of their buddies, pals, friends, and relatives.

I implore you to be proactive and force recognition of your rights. Don't sit idly by while others dictate your future. That might have been the usual procedure in times past. Do what Andy and Amy did. As previously indicated, silence in response to these acts is more than complacency; it is acquiescence. Fight for your rights and never give up!

12

EPILOGUE TO PART 2

I once wrote an article published in the magazine of the administrators' and supervisors' association of the state. The theme of the article was generally the basic thesis of this book. A person who strives to make public schools better places in terms of instructional intensity, climate and cultural propriety, and standards-based consistency should rise to the top. This is less about self-promotion than it is about the surest way to create and maintain an educational structure that has the best chance of creating student achievement. If the experience and credentials of professionals are indicative of the likelihood of success in public schools, then those with superior experience and credentials should lead the schools.

If school boards continue to hire, promote, and elevate their friends, neighbors, relatives, and fellow travelers to positions of authority, those passed over who are more qualified will suffer, but no one will suffer more than those whose well-being and educational achievement we are charged with supporting: the students. I fear this practice will continue until the powers that be refuse to countenance it.

The identifying and "calling out" of favoritism, bias, unfair dealings, and discrimination in whatever form shouldn't be considered a feel-good undertaking. In other words, one should not be misled into the proposition that the advancing of a complaint of discrimination is a personal undertaking. It is a public and social obligation.

I charge you to advance as far as you can. Reach beyond your grasp. Acquire knowledge, education, and experience. Do this for your society, community, family, students—and most of all, for yourself.

APPENDIX A

MY TEACHING PHILOSOPHY

I believe the skills and attributes necessary to be an outstanding teacher are the ability to engender excitement in the classroom. The outstanding teacher is an innovator of excitement. The teacher in this day is bombarded with the competing interests of iPads, cell phones, and other entities able to provide immediate excitement and interest to students. The outstanding teacher recognizes this obstacle, plans for it, and overcomes it with his or her overwhelming imagination. He or she sometimes elicits these very entities to bring interest to the classroom.

As a continuation of the foregoing, the outstanding teacher doesn't avoid technology but enthusiastically accepts, understands, and uses it. He or she recognizes that these devices aren't leaving the scene and are almost 100 percent within the repertoire of every student he or she is likely to encounter. These items must meld into any meaningful classroom activity and must be used to enhance the academic performance of the student. The media center must be a significant tool in the arsenal of the outstanding teacher.

Finally, the outstanding teacher is accessible but not pushy. This teacher must be available to the student and other teachers seeking his or her counsel. He or she must be active in school activities and not dedicated to hearing the sound of the closing bell. The outstanding teacher has a delightful presence but a dedicated demeanor. This teacher doesn't suffer foolishness and isn't easily angered. This teacher would rather counsel than scold. This teacher would rather suggest than order. This teacher would rather make something available than force.

In sum, my teaching philosophy is embedded in the positive actions of the instructional professional who is dedicated to students, the school, and the profession.

APPENDIX B

MY PLAN TO ENGAGE PARENTS AND THE COMMUNITY

The strategies I would use to build and maintain active parent and community engagement in the educational process would primarily be extracurricular in nature. In late August or early September, I would sit down with building administration and my parent-teacher association; we would discuss possible programs to implement during the school year.

September

We plan our "Back-to-School" night, when parents will come to school, meet with me, and become acquainted with the program, policies, and procedures of my class. Contact information will be exchanged.

October

I, along with other teachers and school administration, will plan for Halloween festivities. Our school, with the help of the PTA, will design the school to provide apple dunking, scary movies, dancing, good food, games, face painting, and many other activities. Parents and children will come to the school dressed in their most spooky or funny costumes and enjoy. We will, of course, be respectful of those who wish to forego involvement in such activities and have separate plans and activities available for them.

November

We will have a mock election in class and create a lesson that will culminate in "Election Day," when students will enjoy political speeches given by students to advocate for candidates of their choice and cast their ballots.

December

Parents will be invited to a pre-holiday, in-class party respectful of all holidays. Treats and "goodies" will be provided along with holiday music and good wishes.

February

We will have an in-class "Diversity Celebration," during which we will express acknowledgment of advocate for the enjoyment and celebration of the different ethnicities in our class. Students will prepare posters of the country from which their mom and dad emigrated. They will dress in cultural garb, and an entire week will be devoted to the celebration of cultural differences and similarities.

March

Our class will have an ongoing theme for the month: the welcome of spring. We will discuss the blooming of flowers, the extension of daylight, the warming of weather, and the holidays coming up that welcome spring. Students will become acquainted with the changes incumbent with the seasonal change, and we as a class will plan activities to be undertaken outdoors.

April

Our class, with the permission of the building administration, will emerge from the building and have lessons outdoors on favorable days. We will observe the flora and fauna that will be emerging and discuss these.

May

We will commence discussions about the end of the school year and what will be necessary for the students to move to the next grade. Many discussions will be held regarding student responsibility for their advancement to the next grade. Parent contact will be redoubled, especially for troubled and problematic children.

June

This month includes book and materials collection, moving-up ceremonies, locker clean outs, and all other end-of-year activities.

APPENDIX C

THE INTEGRATION OF ENGLISH LANGUAGE LEARNERS AS WELL AS GIFTED, TALENTED, AND DISABLED STUDENTS IN THE CLASSROOM

I believe in the philosophy of "whole instruction." This merely means the educational process belongs to and must involve not only mainstream learners. But it must redouble efforts to inculcate the expansive educational opportunity to all learners, including children who have special needs, those whose primary language isn't English, those who are gifted, and those who find themselves in situations of abject poverty. The curriculum must be inclusive of these learners. To the extent that it doesn't reflect the needs of these learners, I wouldn't hesitate to modify the curriculum.

In considering a modification of the curriculum, I would address the integration of the needs of English-language learners; special education, free, and reduced lunch students; and gifted students by concentrating on four central areas: the creation of a shared vision, the recognition of the need for resources, significant support systems, and the creation of a culture of inclusion within the school and district.

Vision

The actual stakeholders and professional providers must recognize the need to deliver services that include all special children. They must agree on a service-delivery model that is inclusive of the different specialties. The process of planning for inclusion must include all teachers, and all must be encouraged to participate. A supportive administration is very important. This means an administration that is open to and demanding of inclusion and allows for creative exploration in the formulation of the model.

Resources

The inclusive approach to education requires in-service support and workshops for the technical and mechanical creation of the model and the maintenance of inclusive approaches to education. Professional development is key and should be expanded to include after-school, in-service programs on a weekly or even biweekly basis. District-sponsored workshops would also enhance the creation of meaningful integration. Every professional should have an idea regarding different types of support and should constantly be thinking of different service delivery systems.

Support Structures

In a discussion of support structures whose purpose is the creation of a meaningful inclusion system, the paraprofessionals and resource teachers must be recognized as invaluable. The teachers cannot hope to create a meaningful system or elevate a languishing one without these professionals. Additionally, there must be recognition of the need for more trained personnel in the classroom, the opportunity for collaboration, administrative support, planning, and teaming. The paraprofessionals would work with small groups and must be well trained but could provide significant support to the teachers, especially when supervised closely by the professionals.

It's important that support services for students in an inclusion situation be provided in the same room. The stigma of having to be removed to a different room for these services is the definition of an anti-inclusion operation. Additionally, the provision of these services in the regular classroom allows for greater flexibility in the delivery of these services. The collaboration of the paraprofessional and resource teacher with the regular education teacher would be optimal for the provision of small group instruction and duplicative in allowing for the maximization of key individual instruction. With such a setup, as students' needs change, the composition of the small groups could change.

The Culture of Inclusion

Inclusive education must be a familiar part of everyday life in school. There must be a clear and unequivocal definition of inclusion on the lips of every professional and staff member in the school. It should be posted, obvious, and recognizable in the most accessible place in the school building, preferably as soon as a person walks through the main entrance. A solid definition could define inclusion as a classroom of children with a range of abilities and backgrounds. It isn't just the placement of a child with a disability in a regular classroom setting. Some of these students are English language learners; some are at-risk students. The inclusive classroom must be the norm, not the exception. There should be no isolation of students with diverse learning challenges. The teachers in such an environment must be resources for each other and be prepared and able to share teaching strategies and ideas as to how best to use resource teachers and paraprofessionals.

In conclusion, professionals, administrators, and other stakeholders must be responsible for and involved in the creation of the curriculum. Without knowledge of the necessity for the inclusion of a diverse population of students, a meaningful curriculum cannot be created. The curriculum is not a by-product of a desire for inclusion; it is an inextricable element of inclusion, for a meaningful curriculum can only enhance the philosophy of inclusion, whereas a pointless one will not only aid in the end result of inclusion but may also actually work adversely on its precepts.

APPENDIX D

WHAT PERSONAL CHARACTERISTICS DEFINE AN EXCELLENT TEACHER?

The excellent teacher is technically proficient, empathic to colleagues, mindful of the stakeholders in education, and knowledgeable of the product being produced and the need for excellence in that product. This teacher is tactically and technically proficient and thereby cognizant of the situation all teachers must endure and be prepared to address.

The excellent teacher must realize that, as in any organization, there is a hierarchy. The teacher is a leader and responsible for the efficient operation of the classroom. That doesn't mean the classroom is an island or monolith. The teacher must recognize the school administration, the academic standards to be addressed and met, and the school district policies, practices, and procedures. The quality teacher instills in students a pride and sense of self-worth that will make them do what is necessary without having to be told to do so.

The excellent teacher is something of a politician, constantly interfacing with parents, students, fellow teachers, and anyone else who has a stake in the education of young people. He or she is a listener and is always receptive to advice and even criticism for the sake of the organization.

The product the teacher is producing is a well-rounded, educated young person. He or she marshals all the elements that will enable this product to come to fruition. If there is an indication that the product is inferior, he or she will spare no expense and withhold no effort to ascertain where the problem is, eliminate or correct it, and constantly monitor it. The excellent teacher has an active quality-control effort in his or her classroom.

The excellent teacher is dedicated to education. He or she requires the expansion of knowledge not only in his or her students but also in the professional with which he or she works, the parents and guardians of the young people in his or her charge, and the community itself. Most importantly, the excellent teacher requires the expansion of his or her own knowledge, for a limitation thereof will ultimately result in a diminution of the quality of overall instruction.

Professional development, academic achievement, and character training are the particular interests of the excellent teacher, and he or she intermeshes each of these into a single entity, which results in a noble and honorable citizenry of his or her students.

APPENDIX E

HOW IMPORTANT IS TECHNOLOGY IN EDUCATION? WHAT TECHNOLOGY ARE YOU CONVERSANT WITH AND ABLE TO CONTRIBUTE TO?

Technology is indispensable in education. After all, the facilitation of the acquisition of knowledge is the goal. The problematic issue with technology, however, is its ability to distract from the ultimate mission of education. With social networking sites abounding, students can easily find themselves concentrating on the wrong thing. Emphasis on appropriate platforms and encouragement can mitigate this problem.

As a matter of philosophy, we must not avoid the many technologically based entities students are dedicated to; we must accept and use them. The appropriate attitude is to use technology to eliminate paperwork and bulky textbooks. We must also acknowledge that state-administered assessments are being administered and taken by computer. We must gear our teaching methods toward technology. We must also introduce keyboarding into the curriculum.

I am familiar with _____, which includes _____and _____. I am somewhat familiar with _____. I am willing to learn the many different technological devices and platforms and would dedicate myself to professional development in this area.

APPENDIX F

WHAT DO YOU BELIEVE ARE THE QUALITIES AND ATTRIBUTES OF A SUCCESSFUL SCHOOL ADMINISTRATOR?

In my opinion, the successful administrator is a philosophical pragmatist, an innovator by necessity, and a leader by example. He or she is a mechanic—devoted to getting things done but not exclusively wedded to grand opinions involving nebulous points of view that quote ancient architects of pedagogy. Rather, he or she must be more adept at accepting a withering criticism from a parent in the office, a disorderly debate in the school board meeting, the illegal gesture of a local merchant who subtly suggests the use of his goods and/or services for the betterment of the school and/or district, or a student who believes the curriculum is sexist.

I believe the skills or attributes necessary to be an outstanding administrator also involve the ability to engender excitement in the district, school, and classroom. The outstanding administrator is an innovator of excitement. He or she can empathize with the teacher. The teacher in this day is bombarded with the competing interests of iPads, cell phones, and other entities able to provide immediate excitement and interest to the student. The outstanding administrator recognizes this obstacle the teacher faces, plans for it, and overcomes it with his or her overwhelming imagination. He or she sometimes elicits these very entities to bring interest to the classroom and to offset their inexorable ability to thwart the educational process from its true purpose.

As a continuation of the foregoing, the outstanding administrator doesn't avoid technology but enthusiastically accepts, understands, and uses it. He or she recognizes that these entities are not leaving the scene and are almost 100 percent within the repertoire of every student he or she is likely to encounter. He or she also recognizes the effect these items have on the professionals in the school and the district, not only for their personal use but to enhance their ability to impart a meaningful educational experience to the student. He or she recognizes that these items must meld into any meaningful classroom activity and must be used to enhance the students' academic performance. The outstanding administrator recognizes that the media center is and must be a significant tool in the teacher's arsenal.

The professional development of staff members must always be part of the life of the administrator. Proficiency in the creation of our product is possible only by means of constant enhancement in the training and quality control of our production system. The administrator must be ever mindful of the training of personnel. It cannot be disputed that the Danielson Model of Evaluation is a revolution in evaluation, and the use of rubrics and measurements in those rubrics are at the cornerstone of the creation of a proficient or highly proficient teacher.

Finally, the outstanding administrator is accessible to the community. He or she must be available to the student and the parent and teachers seeking his or her counsel. He or she must be active in school activities and not be dedicated to hours of operation in the performance of his or her obligations. The administrator can be said to be a certified politician. This is because, notwithstanding his or her professional credentials, he or she is ultimately dedicated to getting the job done and seeking compromise in very difficult situations. The outstanding administrator has a delightful presence but a dedicated demeanor. This person doesn't suffer foolishness but is not easily angered. This person would rather counsel than scold. This person would rather suggest than order. This person would rather make a conciliatory tone available than force a disagreeable atmosphere.

ABOUT THE AUTHOR

Larry Plummer was born in New York City and is a product of New York City and New Jersey public schools. After graduation from high school, he enrolled in Fairleigh Dickinson University and graduated with a BA in English/secondary education. He enlisted in the US Army as a private; two years later, he graduated from Officer Candidate School and left active duty as a second lieutenant. He entered the army reserves and enrolled in Seton Hall University School of Law. He graduated with a JD and became an assistant deputy public defender. He served in this position for five years, then left to enter the private practice of law. He specialized in school and education law.

After ten years in private practice, Dr. Plummer entered the full-time profession of pedagogy. He returned to school and obtained his MA in educational administration and supervision and his EdD in educational leadership from Kean University. He served for a year as a substitute teacher, four months as a part-time teacher, and eight years as a teacher of language arts. He was elevated to vice principal and served in this capacity for five years in high school, three years in middle school, and one year in elementary school. He was then made a principal and served as such for eight years.

Dr. Plummer has mentored new and junior educators. As an attorney, he has tried more than one hundred cases and at one time was a certified criminal trial attorney in New Jersey. He maintains a part-time practice, primarily involving himself in writing briefs and memoranda of law. He is a member of the New Jersey State Bar Association, the school law section.

Dr. Plummer is an educational consultant who is in demand as a classroom management and differentiated instructor authority and a motivational speaker. You can learn more about him at this website: Outreachteam.com.

Printed in the United States
by Baker & Taylor Publisher Services